I N
MEDITERRANEAN SEA
Oran
Oujda
IDDLE
ATLAS
OULOUYA RIVER
ALGERIA
0
50
100
SAHARA
Toumliline

BENEDICTINE AND MOOR

BENEDICTINE AND MOOR

A Christian Adventure in Moslem Morocco

by PETER BEACH

and WILLIAM DUNPHY

Introduction by REV. JOHN La FARGE, S.J.

HOLT, RINEHART AND WINSTON NEW YORK

CB-B2N
BeB

Published simultaneously in Canada by Holt, Rinehart and Winston of Canada, Limited

FIRST EDITION

Library of Congress Catalog Card Number: 60-12011

Nihil obstat: Paul E. McKeever, S.T.D.
Censor Librorum

Imprimatur: Walter P. Kellenberg, D.D.
Bishop of Rockville Centre
May 13, 1960

The nihil obstat and imprimatur are official declarations that a book or pamphlet is free of doctrinal or moral error. No implication is contained therein that those who have granted the nihil obstat and imprimatur agree with the contents, opinions or statements expressed.

80851-0110

Printed in the United States of America

To Susan, mother of five, and Kathleen, mother of six, who have graciously offered to write the next book while we stay home with the children.

—The Authors

INTRODUCTION

The monastery of Toumliline is a house of prayer and peace in the heart of the Maghreb, Islam's historic center in North Africa. Twenty contemplative Benedictine monks of En-Calcat, in Southern France, came in 1952 to this fountain in the heart of the Middle Atlas mountains with no preconceived ideas as to what form their work might take. They settled in a completely non-Christian territory, with Berber shepherds and small farmers as their neighbors. Expecting no converts to Christianity, they continued their full monastic life. Out of this project grew Toumliline's annual series of international conferences. These are made possible by the farseeing direction of the monastery's enterprising Prior, Dom Denis Martin and his assistant, Dom Placide Pernot. The conferences were aided by the taste and genius shown in equipping the physical and cultural setting and by the cooperation of the monastery's many friends, near and far, as well as by the high patronage of His Majesty King Mohammed V of Morocco and distinguished officials of his government.

At my own visit to Toumliline, in the summer of 1958, I was deeply impressed by the way this entire enterprise, with its many ramifications, turns upon two age-old hinges:

divinely motivated faith and divinely inspired charity. This faith in a crucified Christ, unceasing worship of a Triune God, is practiced in a non-Christian world, practiced quietly and openly. The doors of the monastery chapel are wide open, its hourly *Opus Dei,* the "work of God" or divine service, is public property. The monks do patient manual toil among peoples to whom such work by learned, cultivated men, is foreign. They practice their charity in the troubled spiritual atmosphere of contemporary Africa, where problems of human division are steadily piling up on every horizon. All the fundamentals—religions, social organism, economy, family relationships—"and many others interlocked, are today in process of swifter change in Africa," says an outstanding Protestant missionary and veteran student of Africa, Dr. Emory Ross, "among more millions of people . . . than has ever been known before."

When you travel by plane on a bright summer day, you are often fascinated in watching the huge, radiantly white cumulus clouds as they drift by your window. If you are new to such travel, you have a sense of having invaded a strange world with its grotesque shapes and suggestion of increasing accumulations and gathering storms. Yet the clouds are but a symptom. The real forces are invisible columns of heated air that rise from the ground far below, and become noticeable only when they encounter the cooler upper atmosphere. The daily press today is full of storm clouds that hang and drift over emergent Africa: glittering with radiant hopes, yet menacing as political thunderheads gather and coalesce and harbor dread flashes of racial and religious hatred. As in the case of the physical world, the real forces are unseen. They lie in the invisible realms of human thought and emotion. Only the grace of the Holy Spirit can reach into the hidden realms where these vortices germinate. It is Toumliline's idea to bring the grace of the Holy Spirit to bear upon this increasing menace of conflicting human aspirations, by encouraging a free dialogue of minds linked together—despite profound differences—by a fundamental concern for man and for the Divine Law in its application to human affairs.

As their directors have been most careful to point out, the international conferences do not in any way favor a spirit of syncretism—a minimizing or compromising of essential and irreconcilable differences. Christians, Jews, and Moslems confer neither arguing their basic beliefs, nor attempting to water them down.

The significance of the meetings at Toumliline is aided by the favorable atmosphere in which they are conducted. In the first place, they are a joint conference of Moslems and non-Moslems, on matters of common interest, held in an atmosphere of entire and mutual good faith. It is not merely a question of being willing to converse with one another, but something deeper: a conviction on the part of each participant that those of the opposing faiths have something to contribute toward unraveling problems common to themselves and to the world. The participants, therefore, are intellectually *present* to one another, in the finest meaning of such a word.

But their mutual presence is made possible by another presence, that of the living Church, in the persons of the monastic community, as their host, as their companion, as a continual wellspring of prayer, worship, ceaseless labor—hard, manual labor as well as intellectual toil—and overflowing charity. The *Mysterium Dei,* the Divine Mystery of liturgical adoration, praise, and Eucharistic Sacrifice, is each day enacted in their midst. Yet it lays claim only by silent invitation, not by compulsion or exhortation. In the midst of the harsh and cruelly contradictory problems of the North African and Middle Eastern world a divine and visible Work is performed.

The friends of Toumliline are under the impression that this haven of peace, piety, and perfect hospitality will become a sort of crossroads for the study and discussion of the deeper problems of all Africa.

The conferences do not rely upon some magic formula or sudden adoption of absolute virtue. They do not attempt to reform new legislatures, reconcile labor and management, or banish communism overnight. They do not expect sudden change, or dramatize the meeting of persons of widely differing class, nationality, or religion, or promise immediate divine guidance. Their outcome, whatever it may be, resides in the gentle operation of the Holy Spirit, who often sows in men's hearts seeds that will fructify only long after they are dead and gone. In the meanwhile, their visitors help to cultivate a fragrant garden of wisdom. "As I watch Brother Jean-Michel, the gardener," said a young Moslem professor to me one day, "I see God's hand at work. These are true men of God." That knowledge, it seems to me, is enough to justify places like Toumliline.

JOHN LA FARGE, S.J.

BENEDICTINE AND MOOR

CHAPTER 1

IN 1952 twenty Benedictine monks left the Abbey of En-Calcat in southwestern France and sailed to Casablanca, Morocco. They went 150 miles inland and stopped. Near the Berber town of Azrou, on a plateau in the Middle Atlas Mountains, they built a monastery and called it the Priory of Christ the King. In time, the monastery came to be known only as Toumliline, the name of a nearby spring.

The terrain around the monastery was rugged. It was studded with mountain tops and was alive in early year with grass and flowers and grey, slow-moving masses of sheep. It was a place of bright sunshine and strong winds and of low-flying cumulus clouds that scudded across valleys and scrambled over peaks on the way south to the Sahara.

Settling in Morocco the twenty created the only community of Christian monks in Moslem North Africa.

Why had they left En-Calcat?

They left because they were ordered to Morocco by their Abbot . . . because they were invited to Morocco repeatedly by the Archbishop of the country . . . because they were specifically asked to settle in the land of the Moors by Pope Pius XII.

The monks had arrived in Morocco at a bad time. The country was on the verge of revolting against France. In fact, Morocco's struggle for independence and the crisis of conscience this created for many Frenchmen closely parallels the tragedy today in Algeria.

And yet the monks had arrived in Morocco at a good time, too, for the political upheaval ahead gave them a chance to prove, as one Moslem said, that "all Frenchmen are not evil."

And the monks did prove this in a hundred ways. They did it, for example, by giving tea to political prisoners of the French in the face of orders that forbade all contact with them. The word spread: "The monks of Toumliline are men of God! They are true Moslems!"

With the same spirit that has animated the Benedictine Order for more than fourteen hundred years, the monks built a clinic for the Berbers who lived in the mountains around the monastery, started an orphanage for Moslem children, began farm cooperatives for their Moslem neighbors, created a hospice for Moslem students, and for these same students instituted an annual international summer seminar, which Professor F. S. C. Northrop, of Yale, called, "one of the most constructive developments in the contemporary world."

And through it all the monks never proselytized, maintaining that their work was to be Christians and nothing more. Thus the heir of the Sultan of Morocco could say to the children of Azrou: "Trust these fathers: for even as your own fathers, they will teach you nothing but good."

This then is Toumliline today, a community of strict contemplatives shaped by circumstance into a powerful instrument for social good in Morocco.

But the story of Toumliline is much more than a report of good deeds done by good men. It is the story of twenty brave Benedictines who kept their integrity and identity as Christians and monks in a Moslem land in spite of dangers and threats and pressures.

It is the story of Dom Marie de Floris, the Abbot of En-Calcat, who gave shelter to hundreds of hunted men and women during World War II.

It is the story of Brother Jean-Michel Reder who spent the war years forging identity papers for Jews in Amsterdam.

It is the story of Dom Aimé Tessier who quietly finished his lunch while a band of Berbers argued how they would kill him.

It is the story of Dom Gilbert Combes who was told by a Berber horseman, "Soon we will kill all Frenchmen."

But the story of Toumliline is especially the story of Dom Denis Martin, who headed the monastery from the beginning and who once defied and threatened the High Command of the French Army when an attempt was made to draft some of his monks.

Dom Denis Martin, born Pierre Martin, is a rather tall, large-nosed, wide-shouldered, big-chested man with light blue eyes shielded by bristling eyebrows. The impression he gives is both of repose and alertness. A simple man, he is at the same time a complete sophisticate. He is a gentle person, capable of unbelievable bluntness. He trusts everyone and trusts no one. By training he is an intellectual, by disposition an artist and doer.

Dom Denis was born in La Rochelle, France, in 1907, the son of a doctor. His parents, he says, "were transformed with joy" at his birth because they had lost three of their children that year. One of his earliest memories is of family outings to a lake near Bordeaux, where he would sit for hours under the hotel window of Claude Debussy as this close friend of his parents practiced the piano. Later, when *soirées* were held at home in La Rochelle or in their Paris apartment, young Pierre always started the evening by playing for the guests. "I remember," he says, "how furious I would get, because just as soon as I finished at the piano my parents would send me to bed."

As he grew older, all Pierre's teachers pointed him toward a career in writing. At 21 he was ambitious, proud, and disappointed. His academic career had been marked by mediocrity, in part because of ill-health, in part because he wrote continuously and with little success.

One day his cousin Gisele introduced him to Abbé Jean-Pierre Altermann, the spiritual adviser of Charles Du Bos and François Mauriac. The meeting changed his life. Père Altermann told him, "My friend, you complicate things. There is only one thing that really matters and that is to love God. You are made for that!" Pierre Martin decided that he might have a vocation. For three years, though, he worked at his writing while half-heartedly investigating the Jesuits, Dominicans, and Franciscans. He went to England for a year and then returned to Paris, still floundering and undecided. In 1931 Father Altermann told Pierre that one of his protégés was being professed at the Abbey of Saint Benedict of En-Calcat and asked him to go along to the ceremony. Martin agreed. "I arrived at En-Calcat," he recalls, "and found the whole place in abominably bad taste, and I knew with certitude and tranquility that this was to be my home."

His novitiate had only begun when his widowed mother died, leaving him to care for his brother Michel, eighteen, and his sister Odile, thirteen. For a time it looked as if Martin would have to leave the monastery, but a dispensation from Rome allowed him to continue at En-Calcat while overseeing the education of his charges. He rented a home in Dourgne, three miles from the monastery, filled it with furniture from his mother's Paris apartment to create a familiar atmosphere, and had Michel and Odile move into it from Paris. For six years Michel and Odile lived there under the direction of a governess their brother had hired, seeing Pierre, now named Denis, one hour every Sunday. Eventually, when they had grown up, both Michel and Odile entered the religious life, the first at En-Calcat, the second at Saint Scholastica, a convent close to the monastery.

Martin's health, which had never been good, somehow thrived under the observance of the Rule of St. Benedict. He took his permanent vows as a Benedictine in 1937, and one year later was ordained a priest. When he was mobilized in 1940, army life made him realize how profoundly he had been transformed by his eight years in the monastery. At the request of his comrades, this monk-turned-artillery-sergeant gave lectures on the tenets and techniques of the Nazis, and when France fell, he led his fellow soldiers in taking a vow to remain true to France and to their Faith. Shortly after this, Dom Denis returned to En-Calcat and to his life as a Benedictine.

A Benedictine is a priest or brother who lives in a cloistered community that follows the "Rule for Monasteries" written about A.D. 530 by the Italian, St. Benedict of Nursia. Each community is self-governing, though it does belong to a congregation that is usually founded along national lines. The sum of these congregations we know as the Benedictine Order.

Today there are twelve Benedictine congregations with 233 monasteries and 11,500 members. This is a far cry from the 37,000 monasteries thriving at the beginning of the fourteenth century, but it is more impressive than the fifty that were surviving in the early 1800's. The reasons for the decline of the Order were the Reformation, the feudal practice of appointing laymen as the heads of monasteries, and the rampant anticlericalism of the French Revolution.

Historically, the Benedictine Order has always been more of a movement than an organization. It is a movement that has shown at various times tremendous creative force. The Benedictines are credited with Christianizing most of Western and Middle Europe, and they are the ones who singlehandedly preserved the literary treasures of the ancient world and passed them on to the nations that evolved out of the shambles of the Roman Empire.

Each Benedictine community considers itself a family.

The family has as its father an abbot (if the community is an abbey) or a prior (if a priory, as is Toumliline). The security of the family is guaranteed by three vows peculiar to the Order—stability, obedience, and conversion of morals.

The vow of stability is a monk's promise that he will stay in the monastery he enters until he dies or is sent to another monastery by his abbot. The vow of obedience is made to the abbot and gives substance to his authority. The vow of conversion of morals is a monk's pledge to persevere in his attempts to advance in virtue.

The life that a Benedictine embraces when he takes his vows is one of prayer and work. He devotes about five hours each day to the chanting of the Divine Office; the remainder of his waking time is spent at work. Since each community is meant to be self-sufficient, the labor of a single monk may vary from instructing a novice in philosophy to harvesting a field of wheat, or to repairing shoes.

But what is it that brings a man to give up family and friends and even country, as did the monks of Toumliline, for the monastic life? What is he after? How does he hope to achieve it?

Part of the answer is in the stirring Prologue of Saint Benedict's Rule. Across the centuries we hear him say:

> Listen, my son, to the precepts of the Master and incline the ear of your heart. Willingly receive and effectively carry out the admonitions of your loving Father, so that by the labor of obedience you may return to Him from whom you have departed by the cloth of disobedience.

> To you, therefore, my words are now addressed, whoever you may be, who are renouncing your own will to do battle under the Lord Christ, the true King, and are taking up the strong, bright armour of obedience.

Another part of the answer can be found in what Abbot Marie de Floris, head of En-Calcat, once said to men just making their vows:

> My friends, why have you come to the monastery? With Saint Benedict, we reply immediately: to hunt for God!
>
> From now on this will be your life: you will be God-hunters!
>
> If someone ever asks you what your profession is, you will be speaking the truth if you say: I am a God-hunter.
>
> More than ever before the world has need of God-hunters, even though it may not understand this, and even though the apparent uselessness of your life scandalizes it.
>
> Hunting God is a great adventure. The means you use are prayer, faith, hope, and charity—devices that often seem contrary to the tendencies of our own nature.
>
> God loves Himself to be searched out. We can truthfully say: You are indeed a hidden God.
>
> Yours is a dangerous adventure. Adventures in the world that go awry can always be corrected. But the adventure that you are starting out on will be utterly disastrous if it ends badly. For if you do not find God in the monastery, everything is lost, defeat is total.

CHAPTER 2

"DON'T worry about me," the young Benedictine novice wrote his parents. "I am at peace. If I am sick, there is the infirmary. If I die, there is the cemetery."

With these words, the founder and first abbot of the Abbey of Saint Benedict of En-Calcat, Dom Romain Banquet, announced in 1882 he had entered a monastery. And although he died a quarter of a century before En-Calcat created Toumliline, Dom Romain might still be considered the father of the Moroccan venture. For this short and powerfully built man with the stern look and the regal stance gave his monks the feeling of being the elite of the Benedictine Order. He filled them with the superb self-confidence that allowed twenty of the community to eventually sail off to Moslem Morocco convinced they could retain the integrity of their monastic life. The image of the Benedictine that Dom Romain held up to his community was of a person completely virile in mind and manner. He thought of the monastery as a place where a man could perfect his manhood, and often said that a monk without courage could do nothing in the service of God.

He believed and taught that Heaven fell only to the violent.

And yet it was more than the discipline of the cloister and the powerful personality of Dom Romain that shaped the monks of En-Calcat and moulded them into material equal to the challenge of Toumliline. For almost all of these men had had their characters tempered by war. In 1914, thirty-three En-Calcat monks voluntarily joined the French Army as soldiers. They did this in spite of the fact that they were then living in banishment in Spain, where they had gone after being driven from their homeland during the last wave of French anticlericalism in 1903. This decision to return to France was in line with a statement made by Dom Romain shortly after the beginning of the war. "My children," he said, "always be French Catholics, French monks, French in Thomistic philosophy, French in Thomistic theology, French in things intellectual, literary, artistic. This is the way to serve the Church." Eleven of the monks of En-Calcat who listened that day to Dom Romain died fighting for the country that had rejected them.

When World War II started, fifty-one monks of En-Calcat—the community had been re-established in France in 1917—answered the call to arms. When the German blitzkrieg smothered France in 1940, forty-four of them returned to the cloister. Of the rest, six remained behind as prisoners of war and ended up in Germany as forced laborers; the fifty-first lay dead at Dunkirk. Finally, with the liberation and limited mobilization, a group of the younger monks joined the advance of General Leclerc's forces into Germany. All of them survived to resume their lives as Benedictines.

World War II did not really end for the monastery until 1948. In the summer of that year the third Abbot of En-Calcat, the thirty-nine-year-old Dom Marie de Floris, stood in the prisoner's dock at the *Palais du Justice* in Paris charged with giving refuge to Frenchmen accused of collaborating with the Germans. Dom Denis Martin, the future head of the Monastery of Toumliline, found himself deeply involved in the incident. This affair capped the years of special training that prepared Dom Denis for the danger that lay ahead in Morocco.

This training started in 1940 when Dom Denis exchanged his army uniform for his Benedictine habit. At that time he was asked by his abbot to reorganize the monastic life of En-Calcat's lay brothers. The task brought him a much clearer understanding of the concept of the Benedictine community as a family.

It had been the custom for centuries to treat these men as second-class monks, even though they took the vows of stability, conversion of morals, and obedience that all Benedictines did. The reason for this inferior status was that the lay brothers were not considered intelligent or cultured enough to profit from the riches of full monastery life. In a radical reform which other Benedictine priories and abbeys in Europe eventually followed, Dom Denis brought these men back into the full life of the community. He had them participate at choir in all the offices of the day and gave them a part in the daily intellectual work at En-Calcat.

While he was working out this reform, Dom Denis was also ordered to write a biography of Dom Romain Banquet, who had died in 1929. The difficulty of the assignment was compounded because Dom Denis could not leave his monastery to track down documentation in Italy and Occupied France. Nonetheless, the priest says,

> the work was a great grace to me. It put me in close contact with the mind of Dom Romain, who had been led little by little by God to make a monastic reform. The work also put me in close touch with the forces that shaped the man and with the sources from which he drew his ideas. Dom Romain's motto was "The Rule, only the Rule, the whole Rule," and he gave me many a key to the understanding of what Saint Benedict had written. Of course, this led me to re-study the sources that Saint Benedict himself had used: the writings of the Fathers of the Desert, Saint Basil, Saint Jerome, Saint Augustine, and Cassian. I read and reread them all with a passion. I wanted to have a complete grasp of the intellectual milieu in which Saint Benedict lived; I wanted to understand the background of his ascetical and mystical thought about the religious life.

The manuscript took two years to complete and today circulates only within En-Calcat. Dom Romain had had his share of disagreements with ecclesiastics over his reforms, and "the work is so intimate," Dom Denis explains, "it would still upset many people on the outside."

The education of the future head of Toumliline took a new turn when the Germans invaded Unoccupied France in 1942. During the next three years literally hundreds of

Allied agents, Jews, escaped prisoners, Communists, Socialists, and Free Masons knocked on the monastery door and asked for refuge. The newly elected Abbot, Dom Marie de Floris, acting mainly through the monk he had appointed Guest Master, took them in and then arranged their escape to freedom. The Guest Master was Dom Denis.

En-Calcat, because it was only seventy-eight miles from the Spanish border, must have seemed an ideal place to those on the run from the Germans. But just how ideal it was is something most of them do not know even today. It was inevitable that the Germans would assume that En-Calcat was giving asylum to their enemies. Time after time they staged surprise raids on the monastery but never found anyone they were looking for. One reason for this was that Dom Marie de Floris had an informer in the Gestapo itself, who always forewarned him of the raids. Dom Marie never learned the identity of the informer, for he contacted the Abbot only through a retired French police officer who was pretending to collaborate with the Germans.

Another reason the Germans never caught Dom Marie or Dom Denis was that the monks had connections with the *Maquis,* and once alerted to an imminent raid, they could clear En-Calcat of people hiding there. Usually this was easy to arrange, since the monastery was a regular meeting place of the leaders of the local *Maquis,* whose base of operations was the Black Mountain, a high, wooded, massive, flat-topped mountain that bordered on En-Calcat.

The relationship between the *Maquis* and the monastery involved much more than the saving of lives. One of the monks, Dom Henri de Morant, was their chaplain. A big-nosed, big-faced, heavy-boned priest, he ended the war with a cassockful of medals and a special citation from the French Government that commented on his "legendary scorn of danger." Another side of the relationship developed simply because the business of the *Maquis* was sabotage and assassination. This involved them in occasional crises of conscience. Their solution in such cases was usually the same—they consulted the Abbot. This always caused Dom Marie intense agony, for, while he willingly gambled with his own life and the lives of his monks in his game of wits with the Germans, he shrank from the function of executioner.

Dom Marie was perfect for the part he played during the war. It demanded the courage of a martyr and the skill of an actor, and he had both in abundance. An immensely self-possessed person, he never questioned his ability to outthink the Germans. The pose he assumed when he talked to his inquisitors was that of the monk too absorbed in monastic affairs to trouble himself with the unpleasantness going on outside. His native calm was interpreted as the cultivated otherworldliness of the monk. And quite aside from the tonsure and black Benedictine habit, his whole presence was that of one not even belonging to the twentieth century. His face seemed lifted from a tapestry. It was marvelously homely and medieval and mobile. His black eyes were deep set, and his nose was short and blunt and had no dip in the bridge. Even his voice did not have a contemporary ring. It was deep and richly modulated. And he carried himself as if he came from another age, walking like a prince sure that every foot of ground he touched either belonged to him or should belong to him.

As accomplished as he was, however, at the game of Gestapo hide-and-seek, he came close to losing his peace of mind at one point during the war. The *Maquis* arrived one night with a problem of conscience they had not been able to resolve. Was it permissible, they asked the Abbot, to blow up a German troop train scheduled to pass through Mazamet, a town twelve miles from En-Calcat? Dom Marie, sick with the thought of dooming hundreds of men to their death, sat for a long time nervously rubbing his forehead. And then before he gave his answer, he insisted his visitors show him documents which proved they were officially connected with the Free French. He knew, of course, that they were; and they were perfectly aware he knew. Nonetheless, they went through the charade, obviously as troubled as the monk. Finally, the Abbot said simply that they did have the right as soldiers to destroy the train. As the *Maquis* filed out of his office, the Abbot turned to Dom Denis and said over and over again, "It was very difficult, it was very difficult."

Of all the episodes in which Dom Denis was involved, the most improbable took place in late 1943. It began when Brother Michel-Benoit, the monastery's seventy-two-year-old Gatekeeper, took the priest aside and told him that two men at the entrance demanded to see the Abbot. Brother Michel-Benoit, an ex-cavalry officer who had covered himself with glory in World War I, pointed out that neither man was French. "They are scared," he added in sign language.

The priest went to the gate to talk to the men. They immediately asked for a place to hide. One of the two identified himself as a German, the other as a Czech. The German, bald-headed and middle-aged, explained that they had escaped the day before from a prison in Castres, nine miles northeast of En-Calcat, during a general break. Without offering any more information, and without ever being asked any, he cryptically announced that he had been saved just in time—his execution had been personally ordered by Hitler. The Czech in turn told of being taken from his home and shipped to France as a laborer. He said that he had escaped and had gotten as far as the Swiss border before his capture. The Czech was young, no more than twenty.

When the men told the priest they were hungry, Dom Denis brought them into the refectory. He watched them as they ate, curious to know how genuine their appetites were. Excusing himself, he next went to a phone and called a priest in Castres, who confirmed the story of a prison break. He then made his report to the Abbot. Dom Marie asked if the men seemed to be telling the truth, and when his Guest Master nodded yes, said to accept them into the monastery. He repeated what he always said on such occasions: "Tell no one."

Brother Michel-Benoit found Dom Denis in the refectory. Speaking once more in sign language, he announced that this time two women were at the gate and that they, too, wanted to see the Abbot. Dom Denis signalled that they should be brought into the parlor.

Without any preliminaries, the older of the two women approached Dom Denis when he walked into the room and said, "I'm a captain in the British Intelligence Service. My friend works for the same organization. Can you hide us?"

The startled priest stared at the self-proclaimed spy, then turned around and closed the door he had just entered.

"You are spies, you say, but what is this to me?"

"We need help. We escaped yesterday from the prison in Castres."

The women hardly looked like escaped prisoners. The one who identified herself as a British captain had on a full-length fur coat and her faced was plastered with rouge and powder. The second woman, who had yet to say a word, wore a dark, tight, tailored suit. She, too, was rouged and powdered. If anything, they had the appearance of prosperous streetwalkers.

"Why did you come *here*?"

"We were told that if we were ever trying to get out of France, this was the place to come. We understand that a number of British agents have hidden out at your monastery."

"If you are agents, why weren't you shot?"

"I don't know," the woman in the fur coat said. "We were caught a week ago and we weren't even questioned."

"Where did you spend the night?"

"In a ditch," the same woman answered.

"In those clothes?"

"We stopped at a farm this morning and told the owner we were hikers and that we would like to clean up and have breakfast."

"He believed you, of course."

"He didn't ask us any questions."

Dom Denis turned to the silent second woman and asked, "What is it you expect me to do?"

"Help us get to England," she replied.

"I was in England once," the priest said. He suddenly switched to English. "I lived in London for almost a year. It was shortly after my father died. I worked for an insurance company in London and I was quite miserable."

The woman smiled and then answered in English, "Some people are not cut out for the insurance business."

"Would you excuse me a moment?" the priest asked.

Leaving the door behind him open, Dom Denis hurried to the refectory where the German and Czech still sat.

"Were there any women in the prison at Castres?"

"Three of them," the German answered. "I heard that two of them were English."

"Did you know their names?"

"One of them was called Maxine, I believe."

Dom Denis then explained that two women who had just come to the monastery claimed they had escaped from Castres. He asked the men if they would walk by the door of the parlor to see if they recognized either of them. He brought the men down the hall and pointed to the parlor. They quickly passed the priest, peeked in as they went by the open door, then looked in again as they returned to Dom Denis.

"Yes," the German whispered, "they were at Castres."

"Go back to the refectory. I'll see you in a little while," Dom Denis said as he walked toward the parlor.

"Which one of you is Maxine?" he asked as he closed the parlor door.

"I am," the woman in the fur coat laughed. She grew serious as she said, "May we stay?"

"Yes. But I don't want any more information from you, and I don't want you to offer any. I think I will be able to arrange to get word to the British you are here. Until they make arrangements for your trip to England, you will stay here."

"Where will we hide?" Maxine asked.

"Hide? You won't have to hide. There's a retreat for women going on at the monastery. You, too, will make a retreat."

"What is a *retreat*?" Maxine wanted to know.

It was the monk's turn to laugh. "Groups of Catholic women occasionally come to the monastery to pray and meditate. You will take your meals with them and lodge in the same guest house. Observe what they do and imitate them."

Maxine and her co-spy, Dom Denis recalls, stayed in the guest house for two months, joining one group of re-treatants after another and becoming "examples of piety to everyone." Finally, the British notified the *Maquis*, who in turn notified Dom Denis that a plane would land on the plateau of the Black Mountain to pick up the women. At the appointed hour, Dom Denis had the women driven in a monastery truck to the landing strip improvised by the *Maquis.* Just as they were about to start on their way, the monk asked the two spies to have a message transmitted over the BBC when they got back to England. He explained that he had to make sure his lines of communications with the British were still intact.

Two days later, a neighbor who had been asked by Dom Denis to monitor the BBC came to the monastery to see the priest.

"I can't make any sense out of it, but I did catch the message you asked me to listen for," he said. He repeated what he had heard: *"Bob ne fait plus pipi au lit,"* which translates "Bob doesn't wet his bed any more."

This incident was one of the many showing the combination of ingenuity and ingenuousness that marked the operations of Dom Denis and Dom Marie during the war. But precisely how cautious Dom Marie had been didn't come home to the future prior of Toumliline until the Germans had been driven from the region of En-Calcat. For seventeen men then emerged from the monastery, all of whom had no legal existence. Dom Denis had been aware of the presence of sixteen of them. What surprised him was that the seventeenth man had been hidden right next to the Abbot's cell for two years without the Abbot ever mentioning it.

Giving refuge to the hunted, however, did not stop for En-Calcat when the war ended. For peace only intensified the search for those who had collaborated with the Germans. Some authorities say as many as 100,000 Frenchmen were killed by other Frenchmen during the war and up through 1948. Officially the count was only 10,000, but this is hard to accept since it embraces an admitted 5,234 *killed* before the Liberation. One figure, though, stands scrutiny—39,000 people were sentenced to prison for collaboration by the courts from 1944 on. The prison of Saint-Michel in Toulouse, 40 miles from En-Calcat, was packed with more than a thousand men and women.

During this period the Communists made their strongest bid for power in France. Their stepping stone was the National Assembly, in which they had the largest representation of any party, 183 out of a total of 618. Alleged rightist plots were constantly being nipped in the bud by the Socialist Minister of the Interior, Edouard Depreux. And while the collaborators were being tracked down, En-Calcat still gave refuge to anyone knocking at its gates, as did other monasteries in France. It was inevitable that Minister Depreux would discover the "Conspiracy of the Soutanes," as he called it. En-Calcat became one of his targets.

Three times the police invaded the monastery looking for collaborators, printing presses, arms. They found nothing. A fourth time the *Sureté Nationale* sent men from Paris and occupied En-Calcat off and on for a week. They arrived March 16, 1946, and immediately posted guards with submachine guns outside the chapel door and watched the monks parade past, hoping to spot a collaborator hidden under a cowl. When they interrogated the Abbot, they demanded to know if it was true that a tunnel connected En-Calcat with the convent of St. Scholastica, three miles away.

"Of course it's true!" de Floris said. "How else can you explain the presence of the Black Mountain? It is the dirt we dug up when we made the tunnel."

The police then went to St. Scholastica and demanded entrance. The nuns refused to let them in. By this time Dom Marie had showed up. "You realize that the nuns are cloistered," he warned them. "If you enter the convent, those Catholics among you, and there must be some, will be automatically excommunicated." The police didn't argue. They returned to En-Calcat and continued their search. Finding nothing, they promised to return the next day.

What happened following their departure was part comedy, part melodrama. For some reason, Dom Floris hesitated to destroy the letters that showed the monastery had in fact given haven to people accused of collaboration. The next morning he thought better of it. He summoned Dom Placide Pernot, a young monk who was to play a major role in the story of Toumliline. Dom Placide enjoyed the assignment the Abbot gave him, as we can tell from his own description of it:

> At about seven in the morning, the Abbot told me he intended to destroy many letters. He rushed through his filing cabinets and gave me handfuls of paper that I piled into several waste baskets. With my booty I rushed to the furnace underneath the monastery church. Paper is hard to burn when it is tight, so I had to take the paper piece by piece and

crumble it before throwing it into the fire. The Abbot had been in such a hurry that among the things he gave me I found several bank notes. I even threw these in. In the middle of my work, someone came to warn me that the police had begun their search. I hurried even faster. At one point I went out to see if the chimney was smoking very much. If it had been, this would have been bad since the heating system was not supposed to be on that time of year. The smoke, however, was not visible. A much greater danger was the smell. Of course, as I was throwing the paper into the furnace, I had to leave the door of the furnace open. Soon the odor of burnt paper began to spread through the basement and into the whole monastery. But these policemen were such blockheads they didn't notice. And when they finally came to the basement, they didn't even see the huge pile of ashes in the furnace!

After the police left this day, the Abbot wrote the regional prefect of police. "For the fourth time since the Liberation, [he said] our abbeys of Dourgne have been visited by the French police. The agents of the *Sureté Nationale* have just invested our monasteries . . . and they have disturbed the entire countryside. And for the fourth time results have been negative. They did not find the legendary tunnel, nor the clandestine printing press, nor a secret radio transmitter, nor the 'malefactors' they looked for." Dom Marie demanded the searches stop.

The letter produced results a month later. On April 21, the Abbot was summoned to Paris by the Ministry of the Interior. Père Hilaire Martin, his secretary, went with him. For four days it was as if they had passed out of existence.

On April 25 the Prior received a call from Paris informing him that both were in Santé Prison in the capital. Two days later Paris papers published a communiqué announcing that "the Abbot of En-Calcat, eighty-six years old (*sic!*), and Dom Hilaire Martin, called to Paris to be questioned on the subject of collaborators pursued by the police, have been imprisoned for having hidden criminals."

The next day a letter arrived from the Abbot. He wrote that the police had not told him what the charges against him were. He told that he was not allowed any information from the outside. He said he loved the solitude and asked for books. "No letters, no visitors," he wrote, "just God." And then he appended a note telling what happened the first night he spent in his cell—the other prisoners at Santé had serenaded him with bawdy Parisian songs. The Abbot reported he had been greatly amused by the "concert."

Dom Denis concluded that the quickest way to get the Abbot and Dom Hilaire out of prison was to compile affidavits from those people who had found refuge in the monastery during the Occupation. The job seemed impossible, since he and the Abbot had deliberately not kept records during the period. The first affidavit, however, was easy to arrange. It came from the Socialist mayor of Dourgne, who in the spring of 1944 had occupied a cell in the monastery while the Gestapo, who had machine-gunned his wife to death, searched the countryside for him.

The mayor, when Dom Denis saw him, agreed to write out a statement. When he finished and handed it to the priest, he told the monk he was still, of course, very angry at En-Calcat. Dom Denis asked why. "You all voted against me!" the mayor shouted.

Within eight days the priest, working from memory and picking up leads as he went, accumulated a dossier of one hundred and fifty affidavits. Only one man who owed his life to the monks refused to acknowledge this in writing, explaining it would be politically inexpedient to do so. Dom turned the documents over to the Minister of Justice, having made beforehand, however, two sets of photographic reproductions. One he sent to Robert Schuman, Minister of Foreign Affairs, the other he kept. One typical statement—it was from a British agent Dom Denis located in Paris—went:

> Not only did you save me, not only did you give me shelter and nourishment, but you did so without posing any conditions. You demanded nothing of me. You did not concern yourself at all with either my political or religious opinions. You did not even ask if I had any. It satisfied you that I appeared to be on the side of right and of truth, that I was a persecuted man.

On May 23rd the Abbot and Dom Hilaire were given provisional release. Dom Hilaire stayed in Paris to make arrangements for their defense while de Floris drove back to En-Calcat. When Floris got out of his car, the monks lined up and embraced him one at a time, then escorted him to his cell chanting the Psalm of Liberation:

> When the Lord gave back Sion her banished sons,
> we walked like men in a dream;
> In every mouth was laughter, joy was on every tongue.

A letter from the Abbot General of the Benedictines of the Primitive Observance, Dom Emmanuel Caronti, was lying on Dom Marie's desk. It congratulated him for having given help to everyone who had come to the monastery. "Your fatherly conduct," it said, "is that which He imposed in the Gospels: charity, charity to all, without distinction based on race or ideas. You have done well to affirm this principle of your life in front of the authorities."

The authorities themselves decided it would be wise to postpone the case as long as possible. Responding at last to the repeated demands of the attorneys representing the two monks, the trial began at 1:15 P.M. on April 16, 1948, eleven months after the release of Dom Marie and Dom Hilaire. The charge against them was that of "having knowingly hidden out persons who had committed a crime or who they knew were being sought for having done so by the courts."

The prosecutor had just gotten to his feet to begin his presentation when a man dashed in the courtroom and asked to speak to the presiding judge, a man named Vinçon. The two men whispered together for a moment, then Vinçon announced to the packed room that the Minister of Justice had directed that the charge against the monks be dropped. The spectators cheered.

The Abbot, however, spoke quietly to the two who represented him, a Monsieur Chresteil and a Monsieur Brachet. Chresteil nodded his head and smiled.

"My clients," Chresteil said to the President of the Court, "practice charity. They do not solicit it."

The prosecutor began his case. He argued that not since

the sixteenth century did the Church have the legal right to grant asylum. Chresteil, when it came his turn, agreed that this was true. But we are assuming, he said, that law is the refuge for all citizens, and when the law of man is suspended by circumstances, as it had been during the early days of the Liberation, the Divine Law nonetheless exists, and the primary part of this law is charity.

The real point in the case emerged: did those accused of collaboration in the first days of the Liberation have a chance to prove their innocence? The judgement of the Court was that they did not. The final decision was acquittal pure and simple.

As one monk commented at the time, the case reaffirmed the right of all men and of all Christians, and especially of priests, to offer hospitality to anyone asking for it, without committing the indiscretion of asking why the person was there.

But what the monk did not know was that the trial ended the years of training the community needed before it was ready for Morocco.

CHAPTER 3

During the post-war years that the monks of En-Calcat practiced—and defended—Benedictine hospitality, they received several overtures to establish a new monastery in the French protectorate of Morocco. The first came from Jean Imberti, president of the powerful Association of French Employers in Morocco and lifelong friend of Dom Denis Martin. In a letter to Father Martin dated February, 1945, he predicted an enormous economic expansion in Morocco. "We are building a new France here in Morocco," he wrote, "a new France that greatly needs Benedictines to help us achieve the dreams of Lyautey."

Indeed the postwar period did see the building of a new France in Morocco. French capitalists, plagued by paralyzing general strikes at home, poured hundreds of millions of dollars worth of investments into the country. The emergence of the Communists as the largest single French political party further encouraged this flood of money. Morocco's mining industry more than doubled its prewar output, making it the world's second in production of phosphate, fifth in manganese, seventh in lead. The port of

Casablanca sprouted glistening white skyscrapers and handled more shipping than Marseilles. French war veterans hurried by the thousands to stake out their claims in Morocco, while patriots at home preached that Morocco must be the showcase of the restored prestige and self-respect of a France humiliated in 1940. The first postwar Resident General of Morocco, appointed by General De Gaulle, proclaimed Morocco "a conservatory of the grandeur of France" and said it had "an exceptional value in demonstrating the place France can and must occupy in the world."

But the new Morocco hardly fulfilled the dreams of Lyautey.

General Louis Hubert Gonzalve Lyautey, conqueror and first Resident General of Morocco, did dream a dream for Morocco. This veteran of colonial wars in Indochina, Madagascar, and Algeria wrote a friend, "I dreamt of creating, of bringing to life countries asleep from the beginning of time. I dreamt of breathing the fire of life into them, of showing them the riches they had but were ignorant of. In Morocco, what a joy there has been in giving them desire, in quickening the blood in their veins."

If Lyautey was right and if at the beginning of the twentieth century Morocco had been asleep, she was soon stirred awake by the game of colonial grab bag in Africa. For Morocco was too rich and too well placed strategically to escape the attention of Europeans. The British wanted control over her because she stood opposite Gibraltar, while the French looked on her as a natural and attractive addition to their North African holdings of Algeria and

Tunisia. Hovering in the background were the Spanish who had fought the Moslem Moors for centuries and wanted to settle old scores.

But it was France that eventually came away with the prize. In a series of secret agreements, she agreed to recognize Italian influence in Tripolitania (Libya) and British influence in Egypt for a free hand in Morocco. These agreements satisfied all parties except Germany which was battling Britain and France for new markets and sources of raw materials. For a time it looked like war. But then in 1906, President Theodore Roosevelt pressured the powers into holding a conference at Algeciras in Spain. Here thirteen nations, including the United States, solemnly affirmed Morocco's independence and territorial integrity.

This maneuver checked France only momentarily. The following year, after the murder of a half-dozen French citizens, France occupied two Moroccan cities, arguing that the Sultan could not maintain order in his own country. When a new Sultan asked the French to withdraw, he was assured that the occupation was only provisional. The discouraged Sultan replied, "Allah called the creation of the world provisional."

Once again Germany protested, and to back up the protest sent a warship to Morocco in 1911. The French in turn traded territory in West Africa for Germany's indifference to happenings in Morocco. Then promising part of the prize to Spain, France took the final step. In March, 1912, their Minister at Tangiers went to Fez and signed a treaty with the Sultan establishing a French protectorate over Morocco.

The "Treaty of Fez" contained only nine articles. In it the Sultan agreed to set up a new Moroccan government incorporating all administrative, judicial, educational, and military reforms the French might suggest. In addition, he gave France complete control over Morocco's internal and external security as well as the right to act as his sole representative in other countries. In return, the French promised to protect the person and throne of the Sultan "against all dangers" and to safeguard the exercise of the Islamic religion and religious institutions.

Riots broke out in Fez following announcement of the treaty. The French countered by calling in General Lyautey to restore order. This improbable mixture of colonial-administrator and military strategist stayed on until 1925 as Morocco's first Resident General.

Lyautey brought to his job a theory of colonial administration formed and refined during years in Indochina and Madagascar. His colonial credo contained three principles: the European cannot substitute himself numerically, but he can control; since in every society there exists a born ruling class, without which nothing can be done, this control must be exercised through that class; military pacification of a country was meaningless unless combined with the building of roads, telegraphs, schools.

This theory of "civilization by conquest" appealed to Lyautey because of his own aristocratic background. But also, as this veteran of many battles with army bureaucracy once remarked, it has special appeal "because it is distasteful to the military mind, which is a powerful argument for its good sense."

He applied his principles to Morocco, a country certainly medieval by European standards. From the eighteenth century a series of militarily weak Sultans had been able to maintain effective control only of the region around the fabled city of Fez and a few coastal settlements. Along the coastal plains and in the Rif and Atlas mountains, authority was exercised by marauding Berber chiefs. Merchants and artisans lived in hundreds of walled towns and paid "protection money" to one or another of these Berbers.

From his years spent in Algeria, Lyautey had an immense admiration for the fiercely independent Berbers. Their way of life, he said, "endows the eye and certain sides of the intelligence with a sharpness that awes Europeans. A Berber tribe is by birth a regiment." Another French General who took part in the conquest of Morocco and later became a Resident General, Augustin Guillaume, paid his Berber opponents this tribute:

> The dominant sentiment in the Berber which eclipses all others, is his innate love of independence. His instinctive horror of all forms of constraint and all domination explains his desperate resistance to foreign penetration. Though deeply attached to his property, the Berber nevertheless does not hesitate to sacrifice it entirely in this struggle. Each one defends his territory to the end with a tenacity which may cause surprise but which compels admiration. As soon as he is old enough to bear arms the Berber takes part in the struggle. Contempt for death stimulates his pride. He is always ready to defend the tribal soil or to rush to the attack at the call of his brethren. He is an incomparable warrior, indisputably the best in North Africa.

No one knows for certain the origin of Morocco's indigenous Berber-speaking people. While only some are blond or red-haired and blue-eyed, almost all have features and complexions similar to the Mediterranean peoples of Spain, Provence, and Italy. There are historians and anthropologists who believe they came from Europe across the Iberian peninsula. Others feel their original home was either the Middle East or West-central Africa.

Some things about the Berbers, however, are certain. One is their ability to assimilate rather than to be assimilated by the waves of invaders punctuating their thirty-two-century-old history. First came the Phoenicians, followed by Carthaginians, the Romans, the Vandals, the Byzantines, the Arabs, and, finally, the French.

Another certainty is the Berbers' ability to do their own invading, explaining an old Berber's recent complaint, "The trouble with people nowadays is they don't like to fight." In the third century B.C., Berber troops fought beside Hannibal when he marched over the Alps and into Italy. A Berber chieftain, Ibn Tarik, led an invasion of Spain in A.D. 711, and gave his name to the Rock of Gibraltar, a corruption of the Arabic *Jebel Tarik* or Tarik's hill. On another occasion, a Berber army brought off the only successful invasion of Egypt from the West, a feat even Rommel's Afrika Korps could not accomplish.

Whereas the Phoenician and Carthaginian invaders stuck close to their coastal trading ports, the Romans moved inland to the rich plains of central Morocco. Ruins exist to this day of the once thriving city of Volubilis, from which Roman legions marched forth to check rebellious Berber tribesmen as far south as the Sahara. One Berber, Juba II, went to school in Rome, married a daughter of Anthony and Cleopatra, and returned a provincial governor.

Since the Berber language has no written form, what we know of the hill people of North Africa during the eight centuries of Roman and Byzantine influence is restricted to vague reports of forces attacking and then withdrawing from the Roman frontiers. The very name we give them today comes from the Roman use of the Greek word *barbaros,* those outside the pale of civilization. These people, however, called themselves *Imazighen*—noble or free men.

Of all the invasions of Morocco, only the Arabic from the seventh to the eleventh centuries and the French in the twentieth century drastically altered the country's history. When the Prophet Mohammed died in A.D. 632, less than half of Arabia itself had accepted Islam. Yet exactly one hundred years later, the Franks under Charles Martel beat off a band of raiding Moslems a hundred miles south of Paris, while 6,000 land miles to the East, Moslems were pushing into India. One Moslem general, Okba ben Nafi, swept across North Africa and captured the last Byzantine stronghold there in A.D. 682. Legend says this same general rode into the Atlantic surf on his white charger, calling on Allah to witness that there were no lands further west to convert to Islam. (The Arabic name for Morocco, *Maghreb el Aksa,* means the land furthest west.)

The Berbers, many with a veneer of Christianity or Judaism over their basically animistic religion, fought back, killing General Okba as he returned from the coast.

Twenty years later another Arab army swept into Morocco, apparently with more success this time, because we find the subsequent Arabic invasion of Spain led by the Berber Ibn Tarik.

The religion of the invaders, Islam, spread slowly but surely among the Berbers, although it was often grafted onto local practices. On the other hand, the political authority of the invaders was challenged time after time by the Berbers. One successful Berber revolt brought on a second Arab invasion that stamped Morocco with the Arabic culture it has to this day, for instead of sending just tens of thousands of armed horsemen, hundreds of thousands of Bedouin men, women and children moved into North Africa. The success of this immense invasion is shown in today's language statistics. Since the Bedouins, like the rains in Spain, stayed mainly in the plains, mountainous Morocco still remains almost fifty per cent Berber-speaking while in accessible Tunisia less than two per cent speak Berber.

Five centuries of successive Arabic and Berber dynasties brought Moroccan culture to full flower. This was the period that developed Moorish architecture, best typified, perhaps, by the Alhambra in Granada. While Europe was emerging from the "dark ages," the Karaouine University in Fez attracted scholars from all over the world. At one point the Moroccan political domain extended from Senegal in West-central Africa to Algiers and across to the Catalonian border in northern Spain.

By the sixteenth century Spanish, Portuguese, and Turkish armies were shutting off Morocco from the rest of the world. This isolation was gradual though, for we find one Sultan, the legendary Moulay Ismail, negotiating to add a daughter of Louis XIV to his harem of 4,000. Another Sultan, Mohammed ben Abdallah, corresponded with the first President of the United States. George Washington sent a copy of our Constitution to the monarch, who in turn established diplomatic relations with the new republic. The Sultan's son later presented the United States with a palace which to this day houses its officials in Tangiers.

Although France managed to wrest control of Algeria and Tunisia from the Ottoman Turks by the end of the nineteenth century, independent Morocco remained a land of mystery. There was some economic penetration of Moroccan ports by European traders, but travel to the interior was impossible without a strong military escort.

This combination of danger and mystery appealed to the jaded appetites of the unpromising twenty-four-year-old Vicomte Charles de Foucauld, then serving with the French Army in Algeria. He asked his superiors for permission to make a reconnaissance mission through Morocco. They turned him down, feeling that a man they once suspended "for lack of discipline and notorious misconduct"—he had tried to pass off one of his mistresses as the Vicomtesse de Foucauld to the society-conscious circle of officers' wives—lacked sufficient character and stability. De Foucauld surprised everyone by resigning his commission and devoting the next eighteen months to a program of physical self-discipline and the study of the Arabic, Berber, and Hebrew languages, astronomy, and the use of geodetic instruments.

He made the eleven-month trip through Morocco in 1883-1884 disguised as a rabbi. To go as a Christian was impossible. To go as a Moslem might mean detection and death. Morocco's Jewish community, however, was segregated in *Mellah* (separate walled quarters) and was engaged in commerce, giving De Foucauld both seclusion and an excuse to travel.

The results of his journey—he narrowly escaped death on several occasions—were published in his *Reconnaissance au Maroc* and contained a wealth of military information. Almost 1,000 of the 1,400 square miles he mapped were mostly blank spaces on French Army maps. Later General Lyautey and his officers were to make use of this book in their conquest of Morocco.

De Foucauld's adventure was much more than a successful intelligence mission. To a friend he wrote: "The sight of the Moslem Faith, of these souls living in the continual presence of God, gave me a glimpse of something vaster and more real than worldly preoccupations." Two years later he became a Trappist monk. He remained, though, concerned about the Moslems and thought of their possible conversion. "The word is much," he said, "but example, love and prayer are a thousand times more. Let us give them the example of a perfect, divine life. Let us love them with that all-powerful love that can make itself loved."

Given permission to leave the Trappists, he lived for three years a solitary life of poverty among the Moslems of the Holy Land. Returning to France where he was ordained priest, De Foucauld resolved to live among the

Moslems of North Africa. He proposed to settle as close as possible to the Moroccan border against the day it was opened up by the French. Although he never again set foot in Morocco, he lived among the Berbers in the Algerian Sahara until murdered by some of them in 1916.

In notes he left, Father de Foucald asked:

> To make the Moslems come to God must one try to excel in certain ways they esteem: for example, in being audacious, a good rider, a good shot, generous in a somewhat lavish way? Or must one practice the Gospel in abjection and poverty, going barefoot and without baggage, working with one's hands, living poorly like a small workman? It is not from the Berbers we must learn to live but from Jesus. The Moslems are not deceived. Of a good rider, a good shot, they say, "He is worthy to be a Berber." But were a missionary to live the life of St. Anthony in the desert, they would say, "He is a saint."

Charles de Foucauld's life and death has inspired many French men and women to share their lives with North Africa's Moslems. He himself dreamed of recruiting lay missionaries who would neither preach nor teach, but would simply show forth Christ in their daily lives. Today, The Little Brothers of the Sacred Heart, founded in 1933, The Little Sisters of the Sacred Heart, and The Little Sisters of Jesus, both founded in 1939, lead lives of contemplation and service while sharing the poverty of their Moslem neighbors. One such group of sisters lives in a Berber tent near Toumliline.

A French Jesuit, Father Guillou, who had gone to Morocco inspired by the ideas of Charles de Foucauld, issued the second invitation to the monks of En-Calcat to come to Morocco. In February, 1947, Father Guillou went to En-Calcat with a proposal for the Abbot, Dom Marie de Floris. He told Dom Marie of his having resigned as Director of the Agricultural School at Angers to recruit agricultural technicians as lay missionaries for Morocco. "I want to create two centers," the Jesuit said. "One, already begun just outside Rabat, will be a center of agricultural life comprising a model farm and a technical school. The other would be a center of spiritual life, preferably a community of Benedictine monks." Father Guillou then offered five hundred acres of land to En-Calcat for the proposed monastery.

The Abbot did not reject the offer out of hand. He mentioned that En-Calcat had already been asked by the Benedictine Bishop of Copenhagen to consider a foundation in Denmark. He further said that no En-Calcat foundation could be tied to any project that would interfere with the contemplative life of his monks. In any event, the Abbot pointed out, assuming the Danish proposal was rejected, those investigations plus the ones on Morocco would mean that it would be at least three years before they could give a final answer.

The prospect of a three-year delay by En-Calcat discouraged a group of wealthy French *colons* and army officers also hoping to see Benedictines in Morocco. They asked Msgr. Amédée Lefèvre, the Archbishop of Rabat, to make arrangements elsewhere, and soon a Benedictine monastery did exist in Morocco. The Abbot of En-Calcat was informed of this and dismissed from his mind the possibility and need of a second foundation.

For a number of reasons the new Moroccan monastery failed. Once again overtures were made to En-Calcat, this time through a good friend stationed in Rabat, Colonel Guillaume de Tournemire. In a letter to the Abbot dated January 29, 1950, the Colonel explained his role as intermediary for the Archbishop of Rabat. Because of the delicate situation following the failure of the first Benedictine community in Morocco, he said that Archbishop Lefèvre would prefer the official initiative for a new foundation to come from En-Calcat. De Tournemire suggested a possible location for a monastery was at a place called Toumliline where a small school for boys was in financial difficulties. If the monks would take over the school, the Colonel wrote, a layman would make them an initial gift of $15,000.

Dom Marie de Floris waited a month before answering De Tournemire's letter. In a chatty note which included news of the academic achievements of the Colonel's son in the monastery school, the Abbot asked for time to think over the invitation. He explained that En-Calcat's investigation of a possible foundation in Denmark would be completed within four or five months. Should they decide against Denmark, he promised, they would at least consider Morocco. There was one prior condition, however. The Abbot insisted there be a full clarification of the status of the monastery that had failed in Morocco, since it had been under the authority of a Benedictine congregation other than his own. He wrote: "We will never agree to take on the odium of establishing a foundation that would be 'the rival' of another. The Golden Rule ought to govern the relations between all honest men, and consequently, I like to believe, the relations between ecclesiastics and monks."

Later as he was discussing with Bishop Johannes Suhr of Copenhagen a possible Danish foundation, a personal message came from Pope Pius XII urging de Floris to attempt the Moroccan foundation. In mid-October, 1950, the Abbot flew to Morocco.

In his notes on the trip Dom Marie de Floris mentions he detected a certain *snobisme* in the desire of many laymen who wanted Benedictines in Morocco. "They have not understood, to hear them speak, the essentials of the monastic vocation and its bearing on a foundation in a Moslem country." But their desire for a foundation was "profound" and, he wondered, "is it absolutely necessary that the laity have grasped and understood these essentials when certain monks themselves have not done so?"

In the first of three conversations with Archbishop Lefèvre, the Abbot of En-Calcat insisted his monks would not accept any ministry which would require them to remain outside the cloister. The Archbishop requested that the new monastery have a guest house where priests and members of Catholic Action groups could come for retreats. A difference developed between them over the location of a monastery. The Archbishop disclaimed the invitation to Toumliline contained in the letter sent by Colonel de Tournemire. While agreeing that the mountainous region of Toumliline was perfect from the standpoint of solitude, climate, and beauty, he felt it was too isolated. He proposed a property along the Atlantic coast between Rabat and Casablanca, the two cities that contained nearly seventy-five per cent of the Catholic population of Morocco. In turn, Dom Marie insisted on a more remote location to insure monastic solitude.

A second interview later the same day took up some of the problems inherited from the earlier Benedictine foundation. Then Msgr. Lefèvre again proposed the coastal location for the En-Calcat foundation. The Abbot felt that the Archbishop's preference in locations was due to his previous experience as chaplain to The Young Christian Workers movement in Paris. Deeply concerned with the social and moral problems of the workingman, the Archbishop was anxious to establish a center of spiritual repose and influence in the vicinity of Casablanca, the commercial and industrial heart of Morocco. Dom Marie was sure he could convince the prelate that such a center and the proposed foundation were not compatible. As the talk finished, the Archbishop passed on an offer by a Catholic layman to give the monks six hundred acres of land and financial support if they would open a "Boys Town." The Abbot rejected the offer immediately and the Archbishop agreed that this seemed wise.

A week later the Abbot had a final interview with Msgr. Lefèvre to summarize the points they agreed on. The Archbishop promised to let the monks lead their monastic life without asking them to perform any ministry incompatible with that life and asked only that they build a guest house for retreatants and that they interest themselves in the spiritual formation of his diocesan clergy. He also asked that de Floris consider building a home for aged priests near the monastery. The Archbishop bluntly admitted that he could offer the monks little in the way of financial support. He said he was delighted, however, with their plans to earn their own living, if they came to North Africa, by manual labor, "an excellent example for the Moroccan people and especially for some Europeans in Morocco." He finally proposed that their disagreement over the location of the new monastery be settled only after a monk sent by the Abbot investigated all possibilities and reported on them. Both men then agreed that the foundation, if it were to be made, be delayed one or even two years. For the Archbishop, the added time might help erase the impression left by the failure of the earlier Benedictine community.

Early in 1951, Dom Marie sent his Cellarer to inspect the locations suggested for the monastery. He recommended Toumliline. In March the same year the Abbot returned to Morocco for final discussions with Msgr. Lefèvre, who now agreed to the Toumliline site. The monks could have the buildings and equipment of Toumliline and the use of its 125 acres of land if they would assume its debts of seven million francs ($20,000). The Abbot returned to En-Calcat on Wednesday of Holy Week wondering where he could get the money.

The problem was actually crucial, for the Abbot knew that En-Calcat could not afford the amount. He was disappointed that one of the laymen he had met in Morocco had not offered to assume the debt. He had assured the anxious Archbishop, however, he would try in every way to get the money, for the Abbot was now the man most convinced that there should be an En-Calcat foundation in Morocco.

Three days later, on Holy Saturday, the Gatekeeper called Dom Marie to say a visitor wanted to see him. The Abbot recognized the tiny grey-haired woman he found in the monastery parlor as the recently widowed Madame Edmond Barbaro of Marseilles. She had a brisk business-like manner.

"Is it true that you intend to start a monastery in Morocco?"

"Yes, but why do you ask?"

"I am interested in such a foundation."

She handed him a small package wrapped in brown paper, shook hands quickly and left. Dom Marie opened the package. Inside he found seven million francs.

During Chapter that night, the monks of En-Calcat voted unanimously in favor of a foundation of Toumliline.

In July, Dom Marie sent his sub-Prior, Pierre de la Jonquière, and another monk-teacher, Jacques de Charry, to Toumliline to run the school inherited with the location and to prepare for the arrival of monks from En-Calcat the following year. Some weeks later the Abbot approached Father Denis Martin.

"I must go to Toumliline tomorrow. I would like your advice on some points, so you will accompany me."

As they drove from the monastery the next morning, the Abbot turned to Father Martin.

"Are you glad to come on the trip?"

"Of course."

"Why?"

"I'm serving you."

The Abbot looked Father Martin in the face. "You do not understand why I am taking you with me?"

The future Prior of Toumliline replied, "I understand now."

CHAPTER 4

THE conversation switched suddenly from the wines of Beaune to insurrection. Colonel Marcel Clesca, commander of the French troops in Azrou looked at Dom Denis and said, "Let me acquaint you, Father, with my plans in the event of a Moroccan uprising. The whole French community in Azrou, civilians and soldiers, will gather in the court of the Berber College and carry on its resistance from there."

It was midmorning August 28, 1952. Dom Denis had arrived at Toumliline late the evening before from En-Calcat, preceding his monks by five weeks. He listened carefully as the pleasant-voiced, sixty-year-old, red-faced Colonel explained the possibilities of revolution in Morocco. When the officer paused, Dom Denis shook his head from side to side.

"There is something you must understand," the priest said quietly. "We will not take refuge in the college or any place else. We shall not leave the monastery."

"Even if it prevented the massacre of your monks?"

"We accept the risk, but in no event will we link our cause with the French Army."

"How will you defend yourselves?"

"We are not people who defend themselves."

"Well, in that case *we* will defend you."

"If you send troops to the monastery, we will hide in the woods. Under *no* condition will I allow myself and my monks to be protected by troops."

Clesca pointed to a town on the map hanging on the wall behind his desk and said, "This is Sétif, in Algeria. Recently two priests were murdered there. And who killed them? Their Moslem servants. You don't *know* these people. They will do the same to you even though you suppose they are your friends."

"It is my choice and my responsibility," Dom Denis insisted. "I wanted you to know my precise position."

"I understand *your* position, but how will your monks feel?"

"My monks? If only you knew them! They ask only one thing, the chance to bear testimony to their faith."

The list of monks assigned by Abbot Marie de Floris to Toumliline had been read at Chapter on July 16. It included twenty men, fifteen priests and five lay brothers. Not counting Dom Denis Martin, the priests were Jean-Marie Martin (no relation to Dom Denis), Fulcran Hebrard, Jacques de Charry, Odon Lacassin, Anselme Foerster, Charles Lyonnet, Aimé Tessier, Mayeul Coquin, Edouard Lebel, Pius Aymard, Victor de Champlouis, Jean de Chabannes, Gilbert Combes, and Ambroise de Tournemire, brother of Colonel Guillaume de Tournemire. The lay brothers were Eugene Carme, Cyprien Doutte, Maurice

Tournier, Jean-Michel Reder and Marie-Antoine Varguet.

The monks had not been chosen on the basis of superior talent. Rather, it was on the conviction that each was completely adjusted to monastic life. Yet each of them did have special qualifications that would allow them to contribute to Toumliline. Land had to be cleared and planted in Morocco, and Dom Aimé, a smiling, humble, and thoroughly stubborn man, had been in charge of the farm at En-Calcat. A library had to be established, and Dom Fulcran was the man to see that this was done right. There had to be a teaching staff at the monastery for the young students at Toumliline and for future novices, and Dom Jean-Marie (named sub-Prior of Toumliline), Jacques, Odon, Fulcran had among them advanced degrees in the sciences, letters, theology, canon law, philosophy. And although none of the monks knew the language of the Berbers, three of them did speak Arabic fluently. They were Dom Gilbert, Dom Ambroise, and Dom Jean, the first one having grown up in Morocco, the other two having spent between them sixteen years in the Middle East. Then, too, a complex of buildings had to be constructed at Toumliline, and the avant-garde architect, Brother Jean-Michel, one of the monks to receive advance notice he was going to Morocco, had been working on blueprints for months.

In a quiet, happy, Benedictine way, each of the monks selected for Morocco was formidable. Each of them had been schooled in privation and danger and had emerged tougher and yet more human for the experience. Each of them had been trained for years in the art of self-discipline, and while in personality the twenty ranged from the naturally reserved to the self-assertive, they all shared a facility for getting along with others and for subordinating themselves to the good of the monastic family.

Of the monks selected by Dom Marie de Floris, perhaps the least typical were Brother Jean-Michel Reder and Dom Fulcran Hebrard. The former, who had come to En-Calcat in 1947, had only been a Catholic since 1944, whereas Dom Fulcran, though he had entered En-Calcat just five years ahead of Brother Jean-Michel, had been a secular priest for twenty years before he became a Benedictine.

Brother Jean-Michel was born in 1913 in Amsterdam, Holland, and was schooled in Berlin. When Hitler came to power he left Germany for England. After a year in Britain, he returned to his family in Holland and began his formal training as an architect. The year he opened an office in Amsterdam, Germany invaded his country. Three times he and a friend tried and three times failed to escape to England. They had already made plans for a fourth attempt when Reder announced without explanation he would stay in Holland. His companion went on alone and reached the safety of the British Isles. The future monk, for his part, went back to Amsterdam, reopened his business office and for the next three and a half years eked out a living designing an occasional house. It did not seem to trouble him that right next door was the headquarters of a German commercial firm busy with shipping Dutch foodstuff to the east. The personnel of the German concern were amused by the bespectacled, skinny, blue-eyed

Dutchman who always addressed them in their own language. They may have even felt a little sorry for him because he worked such long hours.

However, it was not only architecture that occupied Reder. For he was operating a flourishing though entirely unprofitable trade as a forger for the Dutch underground. His specialty was creating identity papers and food cards for Jews in Amsterdam. As a sideline, he guided many of them out of the city to hiding places in the provinces. Those who knew him well realized that it was his love of Jews that had kept him in his homeland. He had grown up among them and did not want to desert them. His concern was, of course, well founded—ninety per cent of the Jewish population in Amsterdam was killed by the Germans during the Occupation.

The future Benedictine had a flair for clandestine work. When the time came that he could not have lights in his office because of a power shortage, he calmly tapped the cable that supplied the German office next door. And when on occasion he was hiding Jews in his own quarters while preparing forgeries for them, he fed them by robbing supplies from his Nazi neighbors. At times, too, his knowledge of German came in especially handy. While returning to Amsterdam on a train after dropping off two Jews at a hideout, he heard two Dutch quislings loudly threaten a woman with arrest by the Gestapo if she didn't cooperate with them. After that, the only sound in the compartment was the weeping of the woman. Suddenly an authoritative voice boomed out in German, "*Nobody* is arrested by the Gestapo unless *I* give the order." The two quislings looked over at Reder—it was he who had spoken—and quickly changed their seats. When the train arrived at its destination, they ran.

When he reached his office that day, he heard that the Germans were searching the area in which he had hidden the two Jews. He felt especially responsible because they were two ancient and helpless women. And then he remembered the oriental cast their features had and this gave him the idea to forge papers identifying them as Indonesians, who were fairly common in the Netherlands. The next morning he was back at the hideout with the documents. He was so proud of the work that he insisted they come back to Amsterdam with him so that he could find rooms for them. Frightened as they were, the women agreed. When they reached the capital, Reder registered them at a relatively elegant hotel, where they stayed right through to the end of the war.

It was toward the middle of 1944 that Reder, now on the run, entered the Church. And when peace came, he told his spiritual adviser that he wanted to enter a monastery. The priest argued against it, saying that the decision should be postponed until he had lived long enough in the world as a Catholic. In 1947 he was vacationing in southern France and happened to visit En-Calcat. He asked if he could stay. Abbot de Floris said yes and put him in the charge of Dom Denis Martin, who was back at his old task of directing the brothers of the community.

The route that Dom Fulcran, the second of the two least typical of the monks, followed to the monastery was longer but more direct than the one taken by Jean-Michel

Reder. Born in 1895 near Montpellier, he had visited the monastery once or twice during his childhood. When he was nineteen, World War I started and he joined the French Marines. On April 25, 1915, fighting at Gallipoli, he lost a leg. After recuperating at Alexandria, he returned home and announced that he wanted to join the Benedictine community at En-Calcat. His parents talked their quiet son into entering, instead, a secular seminary. After ordination, he was attached to a secondary school at Beziers, which is about 30 miles south of Montpellier along the Mediterranean coast. His teaching of mathematics and science was interrupted only by periods of additional university study. Eventually he became head of his school, though he still dreamed of the monastery. His bishop knew of this but wanted the priest to stay where he was. In 1941, Father Hebrard at last formally requested permission to enter En-Calcat. The bishop asked him to wait a year. In 1942 Hebrard repeated his request and this time it was granted. The next year, on November thirteenth, Father Hebrard, taking the name Fulcran, was formally professed as a Benedictine, twenty-seven years after he first expressed his wish to join the Order. And when another nine years rolled along and his name was listed among those assigned to Toumliline, the happiest monk at En-Calcat was Dom Fulcran. He no longer regretted the years outside the cloister. He felt that the adventure ahead would repay him for whatever he might have missed. The tall, thin, limping monk with the blue eyes and the narrow face and the deep, rolling laugh decided he would write down everything the future monks of Toumliline did and saw. And with his chronicle, the oldest man of the twenty showed he was the youngest at heart.

The day before the monks left for Morocco, Dom Fulcran started his history.

> On October third, on the feast day of St. Teresa of the Child Jesus, Father Abbot and Dom Elie left En-Calcat for Port Vendres (on the Mediterranean, close to the Spanish border) to take care of the formalities of our embarkment and to spend a few minutes with the Abbot General who came to see us off. In the evening, at the end of Chapter, we all lined up and received the embraces of our brothers. There were some tears. The Prior put it quite well when he said we are generally not demonstrative, though in our hearts we may weep. Came Compline and complete silence. Despite the curfew, we travelers still had things to take care of.
>
> The night was short and it was difficult to sleep. The bell for Matins rang and we went quickly to the sacristy to celebrate our last Mass at En-Calcat. There was a substantial breakfast. Père Thibaut, who was in charge of serving us, looked over us silently. He served us three, four, and five pancakes and a huge piece of cheese. We went quickly to the yard of the novitiate. The truck was there, the floor loaded with trunks and packing cases all the way to the endgate. Most of our brothers came after Matins to say, without speaking, a last goodby. We left at the scheduled hour, 4:00 A.M. With Dom Jean-Marie, the sub-Prior, we recited Matins, followed by "Benedicamus Domino." Our tongues were untied and we awaited the coming day for Lauds.

The trip to Port Vendres delighted Dom Fulcran. He wrote that after a short stop at Lezignan, "we recited Lauds and awaited the sun for Prime. At Narbonne it lighted the tops of the houses and we prayed to God to bless our day." And then after a sharp turn in the road beyond Argeles, they stopped to eat "before a marvelous satin sea." The monks recited Tierce and "lunched joyously . . . forgetting that we had already feasted shamefully that morning." They arrived at Port Vendres on schedule, met with Dom Marie, and boarded the ship. As soon as they had stowed their luggage in their third-class cabins, they climbed the almost vertical ladders to the deck, timidly at first and then quickly and eagerly. They saw the Abbot General on the pier and waved. At that moment a ship's officer raced madly toward the ship and made it aboard as the gangplank was hauled up. There was a long blast on the ship's horn, "the capstans started to whirl, and the *Azrou,* released from the dock, moved out under its own power. Adieu France!"

Minutes after the *Azrou* cast off at noon, the ship's bell announced lunch and the monks descended to the third-class dining room. The roll of the ship did not prevent them from doing justice to the fare. As soon as coffee was downed, the monks raced to the deck again to catch sight of the Spanish coast: the colors and foliage, the cliffs and lighthouses and villages all excited them as they identified settlements and points of land by a map Dom Jean had brought with him. For a closeup view of the sights, the men used a pair of 7 × 50 binoculars supplied by Dom Odon, who was still back on the mainland preparing his doctoral defense. The afternoon was interrupted only by the canonical hours observed by the monks on the fantail of the ship. Vespers were sung that evening as the lights of Barcelona passed by.

The next morning the monks said their Masses in their cabins, using improvised altars set up on the wash bowls. Later in the day the captain let Dom Jean-Marie take a turn at the wheel. It was something of a climax in the priest's life: he had been an honorary French Navy chaplain for twenty years and had never sailed before. For Dom Fulcran, this first full day aboard ship brought back memories of his last ocean voyage in 1915.

On October Sixth the monks celebrated Mass early so that they would not miss Gibraltar. They breakfasted and hurried on deck. "And there it was!" Fulcran says in his chronicle. "But it was not the profile and this disconcerted us since this was the way it had always been represented in pictures."

The ship moved slowly because it was not due in Tangiers until ten the next morning. Porpoises came alongside, flipped effortlessly out of the water, dove again. The ship hit a fog bank and did not emerge until Gibraltar was far behind. And then: "We were all eyes when we saw the coast of Africa, our new fatherland." Reaching port, the *Azrou* tied up near three American destroyers and an American submarine.

The first thing that caught the monks' attention when they reached shore was a huge banner strung across the front of a hotel that read, "Welcome U.S. Navy!" At the sight of this, Father Jean suggested to the Abbot that *they* send a telegram to the Sultan of Morocco announcing *their* arrival in the country. The Abbot turned down the idea. The monks then divided into two groups, one under Abbot de Floris, the other guided by Dom Jacques. Jacques' group made its way to one of the landmarks of the city, the Sultan's Tangiers palace.

> It was the palace of Sleeping Beauty, [wrote Fulcran]. We went into a garden of dreams, of little walks paved with brick set in the earth in the Roman style. The paths crossed each other under shade trees—thorn apple and bougainvillea. Then there was a second garden which was even more beautiful. In the wall was a loge of complicated and multicolored stucco and chiselled cedar. A path led to a door that opened onto a staircase. We saw a patio worthy of the Arabian Nights. We climbed the staircase and discovered a pool and palm tree that we had seen from the ship, its plumes dominating the whole city.

Leaving the palace, the monks next visited the *medina*, Tangiers' native quarter. They heard singsong voices and looked through a battered brown doorway to see Moslem children reciting verses from the Koran. The Moslem in charge of the class glanced at them once and paid them no further attention. Later, on their way back to the ship, a young Moroccan, seeing Dom Jean, saluted him as "El Presidente" because of his beard.

The ship got underway again at 5:00 A.M. and the *Azrou* pulled out of Tangiers and steered for the Atlantic and the port of Casablanca. The monks again lined the rail. They saw Gibraltar standing to the east; to the northwest, Trafalgar.

Within the hour the ship passed Cape Spartel, the point of land that divides the Atlantic from the Mediterranean. It turned southwest and steamed straight for Casablanca. A haze was on the water and the monks that lined the rail were barely able to make out the shape of another vessel moving on the opposite course. And just as happened when the *Azrou* shoved off from Port Vendres, the dinner bell dispelled sentimental reflections.

> The next morning we were awakened by the silence. [Fulcran writes]. No more wind, no more vibrations. However, we did not cry out like Tartarin "Mercy! We are sinking!" for we had been told we would arrive in Casablanca in the middle of the night and would wait in the roadstead for daylight before entering port. From the deck we contemplated the lights of the big city. We heard the whistle of a locomotive and the distant clatter of a train. After a few minutes we went below to say our Masses in order to be ready to disembark when dawn came.

A crowd greeted the monks as they filed off the ship. Among it were Dom Denis and Colonel de Tournemire. Reporters surrounded the Abbot and one asked, "Why have you come to Morocco?" Dom Marie answered him in a single sentence. "We have come to lead the monastic life." Dom Gilbert then drove off toward Toumliline in the monastery's truck with all the heavy baggage aboard, while the rest of the monks piled into a Peugeot 203, a rented Chevrolet, and a second truck and headed toward Rabat sixty miles away. There they were received by Monsignor Louis Amédée Lefèvre, Vicar Apostolic of Morocco and Archbishop of Rabat. The short, silver-haired prelate embraced each of the monks and then led them into his chapel, where he talked to them of the importance of the day to the Church in Morocco. He then led them into his dining room where "he treated us 'in all humanity' according to the precepts of Christian charity," as Fulcran recorded it. "We paid him honor and then left without delay (for Toumliline), for the road was long."

Their immediate destination was Meknes, ninety miles almost due east of Rabat. Along the route they stopped for lunch in a stand of cork trees, then quickly took to the road again.

> All was new [wrote Fulcran], all was beautiful. We could not get our fill of the cork trees, of the little *noualas* (cone-shaped straw huts). Then came immense fields and finally we saw from afar a city (Meknes) that is all white. We circled the native quarter with its ramparts and an admirable gate and came to the European section of the city where we stopped for gas. Then we started out on the road for Azrou about fifty miles toward the south.

The route took them to a plateau overlooking the rich, rolling farmland that rings Meknes. They went higher still, past austere fields strewn as far as they could see with pitted volcanic rocks. They passed a deserted French fort, which one of the monks at En-Calcat had helped man in 1913. Suddenly they looked to their right and caught sight of the incredible Adarouch Valley. They stared at the view as they descended the plateau—to the very edge of the horizon was an assembly of grey, dead volcanoes rising out of the valley floor. The road led away from the vista and worked its way down from the plateau and deposited the travelers in the Tigrigra Valley of Azrou. "We stopped at a beautiful fountain," said Fulcran, "where a Berber was showering his black horse with buckets of water. We drank, we were insatiable. Evening started to fall. As we approached Azrou, Père Jacques pointed to Toumliline."

The tiled red roof of the building that was to be their home disappeared as they passed through Azrou. The town was alive with Berbers come to celebrate a Moslem feast. The caravan climbed once more for four miles and then stopped on a plateau that hung a thousand feet over the valley they had just driven across. The sun was setting. Thirteen hundred miles from En-Calcat, in the center of a forest of giant cedars and oaks, the new community began Vespers:

O God, come to my aid;
O Lord, make haste to help me. . . .

CHAPTER 5

I REMEMBER the first days [says Father Martin]. We were living in a temporary barrack on the site of a former summer camp. Among the workers who were converting it into a monastery were laborers who came from Tafilalet (an oasis on the edge of the Sahara), stone masons from Meknes, carpenters from Azrou. They were of varied racial origins. Some were Negroes, the descendents of slaves imported from the south. Others were blond and blue-eyed. But most of them had the fine and regular features of the Mediterranean peoples of Spain, Provence, and Italy. One of our monks (Dom Fulcran), originally from Lodeve, a little town in the south of France, remarked that these men used the same proverbs and told the same stories as the people of his own locality. Thus we felt we had never left the Mediterranean world and so would not be strangers here. The picturesque clothing of our new neighbors and their language—Arabic and Berber—did not more than remind us that we were no longer in France. What we were struck by was their gentleness, their respect for the monks as *marabouts.* Manifestly they had a sense of the sacred. Once aware of our monastic silence, they made a

> particular effort not to disturb it. These were people of delicate sensibilities.
>
> How meaningful were these first impressions! How curious we were about these men, still unknown to us, who we felt belonged to a kind of natural aristocracy of a race ancient and at the same time new; these people were stately, dignified, extremely sensitive in their perceptions, subject consequently to swiftly changing moods and yet reserved and guided by ancient traditions. We felt in them a complex past, a rich antiquity which had suddenly undergone a great upheaval through its contact with the West. It was not long before they began to confide in the monks who directed the work, and to ask them for advice. Thus, not only did we learn their problems but little by little we found ourselves engaged in seeking solutions. Our lives were becoming immersed in theirs—with the whole life of their land. And now we were prisoners. . . .

These are the impressions of a man who looks back to October 1952 and remembers only the joy and excitement of his first days at Toumliline. But there was much more than this to recall. There was the hard work, with the monks sweating side by side with the Moroccans as they fought to complete the monastery before the snows came. There was the lack of conveniences and privacy and solitude. Most especially, there was the fear that the military would try to use the monks to strengthen the French political position in the Azrou area.

The first night at Toumliline after supper and after Compline had been chanted, Dom Denis told Abbot de Floris of his talk with Colonel Clesca and of his refusal to be protected by the French soldiers in the event of an uprising. Dom Marie agreed Dom Denis had been right to take the stand he had. The Prior then took out two pages of notes and studied them for a moment.

"There was another incident. The same afternoon after I told Colonel Clesca we would not allow ourselves to be protected by soldiers, we had visitors at the monastery, three young men and three women. Moroccans. I showed them around. They were extremely polite and thanked me before they drove off. Within the hour Colonel Clesca called."

At this point the Prior picked up his notes and started to read.

> Clesca said: "Mon père, you have received some young people at your monastery. I warn you that one of the men is a militant Communist. You do not know this country and the people. So I am at your disposal. Every time you receive someone, you have only to call me and I will tell you who they are."

De Floris smiled as he asked, "And what did you say?"

"I was quite polite. I told him I would receive everybody who comes here without asking who they are. I also said I would not ask anyone for information, especially the military."

"How did he react?"

"He insisted he was only trying to help. But I feel the military are so preoccupied with politics that even though they may want to help us, and I don't doubt it, they also unconsciously want to lead us and use us."

"Naturally. The country is heading for a revolution."

"If there is one, do you think we will survive?"

"I don't know. Perhaps. It will be difficult; but that is one reason I chose you as Prior."

At 2:30 A.M. the next morning, Father Edouard, a lawyer turned Benedictine, crawled out of bed, put on his soutane and hooded scapular and, using a flashlight, steered his way past the cots where the other monks slept and walked through the door into the darkness. He stopped and filled his lungs with the cold air. The bite of it reminded him of the hundred nights he had spent camping in the Maritime Alps, skiing, and climbing. But the sounds here were different, he thought, and the smells different, too. The scent from the cedars and oaks was so much a part of the night he felt that if he reached out he could touch it. It was a musky physical presence. The night itself was an immense silence filled out at the corners with the tread of an animal prowling the mountain side directly in front of him. Leopard? Boar? Jackal? With his mind's eye he looked beyond the mountain and saw the vastness of the African continent that spread to the south. His flashlight picked out the bell that hung from the lowest branch of a squat, green-speckled oak standing a few yards from the door of the barrack. He grabbed the rope tied to the clapper and swung it quickly back and forth: it was time for Matins; the first monastic day had begun at Toumliline.

After sunrise and the singing of Lauds, the monks, as they worked, began to examine their surroundings. They discovered they stood on a fan-shaped, thirty-acre shelf of land that cut into the face of the mountain. The summit of the mountain, trimmed with stunted, twisted oak and cedar, was several hundred feet overhead and blocked out a good part of the southwestern horizon. The front of the shelf dropped ninety feet to the Plain of Ajellab, a thousand acres of meagre grazing land crowded with grey-black basalt boulders. From the plain, in actual fact a plateau, they could look down into the streets of Azrou, a mile below. From Azrou, the main highway to the Sahara wound up the hill, passing a mile east of Toumliline. A *piste* (dirt road) began there, twisted along the side of the hill, turned and ran along the lip of the thirty-acre shelf on which the monastery was located. Past the monastery, it resumed its upward climb along a ridge to a pass that led deeper into the Middle Atlas. About half a mile above the monastery, the road went past a rock spring called Toumliline, a name that was to identify the Benedictine community. Looking out over Azrou, the monks had an unobstructed view of the Tigrigra Valley, which ran east toward the eleven-hundred-year-old city of Fez fifty miles away. From the valley floor rose row on row of mountains, some cone-shaped, some with blunted summits.

The colors of the landscape were sombre, light grays and dark, browns and greens and blacks. And yet the view was totally exhilarating. The sky, so light blue it looked as if it had just been rinsed in rain water, dominated everything. Standing on the shelf, the monks had the impression of guarding the battlements of Berber country.

The history of the area bore out this impression. In the nineteen-twenties and early thirties Azrou had been an advance post of the French Army, which had used the town as a supply depot for a string of forts that ran south through the Middle Atlas. These forts protected the lines of communication with the southeastern part of the country, which spilled over into the Sahara. At one time the Foreign Legion had built a post on the very shelf of land where the monks now were. The function of the post had been to prevent Berbers from riding, as they occasionally did, to the edge of the plain of Ajellab in order to shoot at the French on the streets of Azrou. And although by 1952 the Berbers had long given up this game and satisfied themselves with ambushing an occasional military convoy on its way to one of the Middle Atlas forts, Azrou was on the very edge of what was officially called an "area of inquietude." It was forbidden to travel into the mountains from Azrou after dark. Some roads could not be traveled at all unless the French *Chef de Région* in Meknes gave his permission. In 1952 the military head of the region was Lieutenant General Roger Miquel.

In the post-World War II wave of optimism that caught up the French in Morocco, a business man from Casablanca had decided that the shelf where the Legion post stood was a perfect site for a summer camp. He started a long wooden two-story building somewhat Tudor in style. The job was never completed—he went bankrupt. In 1950 the pastor of the French community in Azrou rented the unfinished building, put in a dormitory and two classrooms on the first floor, then established a school for about thirty wild French boys of high school age, the children of *colons* and Army officers. He was relieved when he found out En-Calcat had not only bought the building but also had agreed to continue the school. The Abbot had made this decision in part because the Archbishop of Rabat requested it, in part because income from the school would help support the new monastery. But the need to board the boys complicated the construction that had to be done at the monastery. Dom Denis and Dom Marie de Floris had decided to let the boys occupy their old dormitory, using the rest of the first floor for a refectory, a Chapter room (i.e., the place where the monks meet and talk over "family" business), and an office and cell for the Prior. It was planned that the loftlike upstairs would be cut up into cells for the community and visiting clerics.

But while the monks had no cells, at least they had a chapel. It had been designed by Brother Jean-Michel. Sub-Prior Jean-Marie, writing back to his younger brother at En-Calcat, described it as "very simple, very modern, very white." And Father Fulcran in his chronicle wrote, "It is really a nice chapel, though, of course, it is only a low-ceilinged hall." Jean-Michel had designed wooden crosses for the small side altars where the monks said their Masses, and these especially caught the eye of Father Fulcran—they looked Merovingian to him. The cross on the main altar was of the same type and had etched on it an extremely abstract praying Christ. The altar itself was a simple wooden table on a cylindrical base, and on the steps that led to it were two large and thick white Moroccan carpets with intricate abstract Berber designs woven into them. Choir stalls took up half the chapel and each of the two sections faced a row of windows. "I see caravans on the dirt road, twisting and turning as they follow the route, and all this is like a projection from the texts of the Old and New Testaments which we are singing in the liturgy," Jean-Marie wrote his brother back in France.

Outside the chapel all was confusion and noise. Fifty to sixty Moroccans labored at Toumliline and though they went calmly and quietly about their work, their entire families would show up at mealtime to prepare food for them. The sound of rocks being chipped and wood sawed and nails hammered blended with the chatter of crying children and gossiping wives and the sizzling of lamb cooking over charcoal fires. When the monks would stop working and file into chapel, they would run an obstacle course of timber and tools and babies and baggage and books. Tired and overworked and overwhelmed, the monks loved every minute of every day.

The monks had arrived on a Tuesday and the following Sunday was the first time they took a deep breath. Father Fulcran describes the day this way:

> October 12. Our first Moroccan Sunday. The men are at work. Among them are, alas, two Europeans. Some visits. We made the porch into parlors (it is outside, but the weather is so pleasant), the same porch where we had unloaded our luggage. Father Abbot insisted that we immediately have the enclosure and yesterday we started to carry the stones for the wall. For the moment the wall consists of a row of stones on the ground, but it is sufficient and we faithfully keep silence outside. I sang the conventual Mass this morning. Incense goes up. The chapel is filled

> with smoke like the Temple on Dedication Day. At lunch Father Abbot tells us it is fitting to rejoice. In honor of the day, Father Gilbert made us some coffee. We go out to drink it in the shade of the oaks above the road. Meanwhile the youngest monks explore the woods. They return full of enthusiasm. They saw a monkey . . . and the colonel who commands at Azrou.
>
> In the evening after supper there is a conference by Father Abbot on a subject he has been developing: the importance of this foundation and our responsibilities. He speaks of the necessity for us to be saints. It is the one and only way for us to reach the natives. Father Gilbert then tells us that he had explained to a Berber about their presence at Toumliline, saying to him that in coming there they had given up country, friends, and relatives. He says this touched the Berber but also scandalized him: "No," the Berber said, "Allah does not ask that, it is not true." Hearing this, Father Abbot then tells us that the future of our foundation depends on our giving. We must be absolutely docile to grace.

The next day the Abbot and Dom Denis left for a meeting to pay their respects to the Caid of Azrou. Afterwards, they went from there to Meknes and Rabat to see the Archbishop. The same day the first rain fell, and this threw the monks into a panic because they feared for the books on the porch. But the rain was light. ("Thank Heavens," wrote Father Fulcran, "God tempers the wind to the shorn lamb and we get away with fright alone.") On Wednesday night the monks held their first Chapter. The same day the monks moved from the student dormitory into their cells, even though the cells had no doors, no glass in the windows, no light. But the love of solitude was strong. The morning following, the Abbot, sick with the flu, and Dom Denis returned from Rabat. As evening fell that day, a Peugeot 203 stopped at the monastery and Fathers Placide, Hugh, and Colomban, sent from En-Calcat to help Toumliline for a while, piled out. They arrived just in time to fill the gap left by Father Abbot, Brother Marie-Antoine, down with fever from overwork, and Father Jean-Marie, who had an abscess on his ankle.

As the days drew closer to the day of inauguration, October Twenty-sixth, it rained much of the time. On the twentieth, the monks finally started taking their meals in the refectory, a spacious room with many huge windows. The same day Father Eugene stopped working because a beam dropped on his foot. Finally on the twenty-fourth, the Abbot, out of patience with the generator, ordered Father Gilbert to go to Meknes and rent one. On the twenty-fifth the young students reported to the monastery and started classes. ("The children are fine," said Father Fulcran, "but they ignore discipline.") That night the monks worked into the night clearing the porch of books and stacking them in huge piles along the walls of the Chapter. Praying for fair weather, they saw the stars hide under an overcast.

And then the twenty-sixth dawned. . . .

"The weather was grand," wrote Father Fulcran. "Many, many people and much friendliness, and God, for Whom we came, was here with us in the person of the Apostolic Delegate." With the Archbishop came Father Albert Peyriguère, a theologian and one of the most remarkable

Frenchmen in North Africa. A bearded man with a trunk and head that looked as if they were carved out of rock, this sixty-six-year-old priest was known as the Hermit of El-Kbab. He had lived among the Berbers for twenty-six years, in fact he was an elder of a Berber tribe. Every day he would say Mass in El-Kbab, and the rest of his time would be spent caring for the sick or handling whatever tribal affairs were assigned him. He was one of the few Frenchmen who knew Berber fluently. Wounded four times during World War I, he was an irascible, erudite, kind, and totally loveable man, revered by the Berbers and feared by the French military.

After the Archbishop and Peyriguère came, the other guests started to arrive. General Roger Miquel and his staff, along with Colonel Clesca and three of his officers, appeared. (Clesca had arranged for five policemen, three of them white-garbed Berber *mokhaznia* with submachine guns, to direct traffic.) At 10:30 A.M. Father Edouard rang the bell and the community assembled around Archbishop Lefèvre, who led them in procession to the door of the chapel where Dom Denis, as head of the new community, greeted him. The procession then went into the chapel singing the antiphon, "Sacerdos et Pontifex." Father Pius played the organ as the community stopped in front of the throne prepared for the Archbishop. Vases of roses were on the main altar and along the window sills. His Excellency blessed the chapel after singing the collect of the day at the altar, then he left, again leading the community in procession. He then proceeded with the blessing of the buildings. After the blessing, the Archbishop said a few words to the community defining their purpose: "neither pastors nor chaplains, but men of prayer." Then followed the High Pontifical Mass. When it came time for Communion, the Archbishop had to break the hosts into three and four and five pieces because he had not expected so many at the Mass. The size of the crowd was too great to allow everyone inside the chapel, and many people heard Mass by looking through the opened windows. Afterwards, dinner was served: hors d'oeuvres, lamb roast, string beans, cheese, and dessert. As the meal was finishing, the Abbot stood up and delivered a quiet talk that caused some tears. He addressed himself first to the entire gathering. "Your presence here," he said, "is a mark of friendship which has cost you time and trouble. In exchange I can hardly give you more than a kind word, the best of gifts, Scripture tells us."

He then told everyone about the visit he and Dom Denis had had with the Pope the previous June.

> I told him of our Moroccan foundation—our desire to reply to the call that the Church has long addressed to monastic communities—to carry into mission countries the stable example of the perfect Christian life. The Pope blessed our plans and our efforts. He assured us he would watch over our beginning through his paternal prayer. Several times he repeated to us, "Prayer and example are the forms most urgently demanded of the apostolate in Moslem countries."

The Abbot then referred to the reason for their apparent delay in deciding to come to Morocco.

> In his spiritual testament [Dom Marie said], the founder of En-Calcat, Dom Romain Banquet, told his sons to "temporize" when the question of a foundation came up. "My children," he recommended, "do not hurry to create a foundation; be prudent, be more than prudent when it comes to a foundation." He said that the most authentic sign of the will of God was the benevolent welcome of the Ordinary.

The Abbot looked directly at the Archbishop as he said, "Concerning the Toumliline foundation, this sign has been amply verified. Not only did you welcome us; not only did you encourage us; you called us."

When it came to refer to General Miquel and Colonel Clesca, he told them politely and firmly that Toumliline would be independent of them. "I thank you for coming," he said to Miquel. "Your presence here proves your personal benevolence and we are touched by it." He went on to say that France, insofar as it wanted to devote itself to the work of education and the solving of "human problems," had every thing to gain from the presence of the Church in Morocco. Turning to Colonel Clesca, he continued his thought:

> And that is why, Colonel, you can be happy about the monks establishing themselves in your territory. Deep down, we come to labor in the same essential work to which you have consecrated your career: to aid man, every man, to improve himself. But we shall work at this in a different manner and on a different plane and in full, reciprocal independence.

Next, he talked of his monks . . . "but with the greatest reserve. Monks love anonymity; they should only leave work without signatures." He promised that the community "would do everything to fulfill what is expected of it." Looking once more at the Archbishop he said,

> the day on which the decision was made to send monks to Morocco, I promised I would not send any of my sons over whose departure I would not weep. I believe I have kept my promise. But I must let you judge this for yourself on the basis of their work. What I can say is that the monks of Toumliline, under the leadership of their prior, who has all my confidence and the confidence of his brothers, reached Morocco with joy, with a lifting of their spirits, with total good-will.

Dom Marie ended up by saying,

> Our whole vocation is summed up in the admirable cry of Isaiah: "*Super muros tuos constitui qui toto die at tota nocte non tacebunt laudare nomen domini.*" On these mountains that dominate the plain where two peoples meet, see one another live, search for understanding, the Church has established her guardians who night and day will not relax from praising the name of the Lord and sending to heaven the powerful prayer of tears and sacrifice.

After the Abbot sat down, the Archbishop "answers very kindly," as Father Fulcran put it. "Then more conversations. At 4:30 P.M., pontifical vespers. Fewer people. Afterwards, His Excellency takes us to the Toumliline point and speaks most openly with Father Abbot and the fathers while smoking cigars and cigarettes. He takes Father Abbot, Father Prior and Dom Pierre to supper at Colonel Clesca's." As they leave the monastery, General

Miquel, and Père Peyriguère are asked to sign the guest book. The General defers to the priest, and Peyriguère writes, "To those who have waited for so long, the great dream of Father de Foucauld has at last become a reality." Miquel then neatly penned the words, "With all my gratitude and admiration."

From the time of the inauguration, things went rather smoothly for the monks. The only unhappy note was struck November Fourth when the Abbot, just about to depart for En-Calcat, informed the community that Father Placide had developed tuberculosis. He told the community that the young monk would stay in a sanitarium at Azrou until the doctors would allow him to return to France. Two days later the Abbot and the monks who had come with him to temporarily help the community at Toumliline departed for home. The same day nine of the priests began classes in Arabic and Berber at the French-Berber College, a move that astounded and somewhat scandalized the French community in Azrou.

The last day of the year was logged in these words by Father Fulcran: "Snowbound. Father Gilbert managed to ski down to Azrou and get food. Very difficult." The next day he wrote: "January 1, 1953, Snow, isolation, and silence." Turning slightly less poetic, he added: "The Colonel has invited Father Prior for cocktails. Excellent reason not to go."

CHAPTER 6

ONE day early in the new year, a small European car pulled up to the monastery. Four tall men stepped from the tiny car with great dignity. With their flowing brown and white robes and turbans, these elderly Moroccans looked like Old Testament patriarchs. Their distinctive turbans informed Father Martin that they were from the Beni M'Guild tribe whose headquarters was Azrou. From the deferential way some Moroccans near the gate saluted them, the Prior guessed they were important officials of the tribe and hurried to open the gate. Introducing himself, he bid them welcome. Each in turn introduced himself and shook hands with Father Martin, adding the characteristic Moslem gesture of touching his own heart and lips.

Sipping glasses of steaming hot mint tea—Father Martin had quickly adopted this traditional Moroccan gesture of hospitality—the guests exchanged pleasantries with the Prior. Father Martin realized that theirs was more than a mere courtesy call and wondered when they would get to the point.

"Why are you here?"

"We came here to live our monastic life."

"Why did you come here to Toumliline?"

"Because we were told to come."

"Who told you?"

"Our superior, the Abbot of En-Calcat, the monastery in which we formerly lived."

"Who pays you?"

"No one pays us, unless you count the contributions of Christians from all over."

"Doesn't the French government or the Resident General pay you?"

"Not at all!"

After the Moroccans left, Father Martin was sure they were not convinced by his denial of official French support and control. One thing was certain: normal relations with either their Moroccan neighbors or the Catholic French community were impossible if the monks were identified with any political position.

Shortly before this conversation an incident took place which revealed to Father Martin how little he knew of the complex political situation in Morocco. It involved the bloody Casablanca riots of December, 1952, coming only six weeks after Toumliline's formal opening. French authorities in that largely European city had ordered police to fire into a crowd of Moroccans demonstrating against the assassination of a Tunisian nationalist by *colon* orders. The ensuing riots lasted for three days as French Legionaires joined the police in suppressing the Moroccans. While official French figures listed thirty-eight Moroccan dead and seventy-nine wounded, eyewitness reports put the

Moroccan casualties closer to one thousand dead and several thousand wounded. Some nuns who lived next door to the police station where the riots began described the event to Father Martin. They insisted that the Moroccan crowd of men, women, and children demonstrating in front of the police station was orderly. It was not until the police suddenly opened fire, they said, that the crowd went wild and stormed the station.

The Prior was shocked by their account and, accompanied by Father Jean-Marie, went to the Casablanca home of an army friend for an explanation of the differing reports. When his friend, a colonel, learned what was troubling the Prior, he picked up the phone and called Rabat to arrange an appointment with the Director of the Interior, M. Vallat. Next morning, seated in the official's spacious office, Father Martin demanded to know what really happened in Casablanca. It was actually a show of French force, the Residency official said. For several years, he explained, nationalist sentiment had been growing steadily, its leaders too bold. "We felt," he said, "that all Morocco was being infected with this disease. At Casablanca we simply lanced its core."

The blood drained from the Prior's face at these words. Father Martin abruptly stood up facing the official and seemed struggling to control himself. Suddenly he slammed his fist on the man's desk and said slowly, "Do not say another word to me." The Prior turned and walked out of the room. Father Jean-Marie hurried to catch up with him while the official sat in stunned silence.

When they had returned to the monastery, Dom Denis

told his monks of the incident and explained to them how necessary it was for him to become one of the best informed men on this complex political picture. "Politics does not interest me, it is not my job," he said. "But I must know what is happening so that people do not use us."

Father Martin was fortunate in being able to call on some of the best possible tutors for his Moroccan political education. For the French point of view he had many friends in different army and administrative circles, including General Jean Olié, deputy of the Resident General, Augustin Guillaume. A cousin, General Marie-Antoine d'Hauteville, who had passed his entire career in Morocco and was administrative head of the Region of Marrakech, came often to Toumliline and sent the Prior regular reports analyzing political developments.

For the Moroccan point of view, Father Martin's source was one of the Sultan's closest advisers, M'Barek Si Bekkai. Introduced by a mutual friend, they soon became close friends, exchanging visits to Toumliline and Sefrou, a nearby town where Si Bekkai was Pasha.

As he listened to his "instructors" and read all the literature he could get on the subject, Father Martin came to believe that the growing French-Moroccan enmity had been generated in part by the outcome of a struggle between two antagonistic French interpretations of the way to run their protectorate. For a while, the views of the first Resident General, Lyautey, prevailed. Lyautey had been captivated by Morocco.

> The more I see of the natives, the longer I live in this country, the more I am convinced of the greatness of this nation. While in other parts of North Africa we found nothing but a society crumbling into dust as a result of former anarchy and lack of power, here, thanks to the permanent power assured by all the dynasties following one another continuously, thanks to the maintenance of essential institutions in spite of revolutions, we found a stable empire and with it a great and beautiful civilization. . . .

General Lyautey wanted to preserve those elements of this traditional Moroccan civilization that were compatible with what he thought to be the realities of the twentieth century. His program of "civilization by conquest" called for a gradual military pacification of Morocco which would carry along a great belt of civilization "like a spreading stain of oil." To accomplish this he favored the concept of indirect French administration along with strengthening and controlling the Moroccan Sultan and his *Maghzen* (government). He proposed to educate a Moroccan elite that would eventually assume control of a country bound to France by the strongest economic and cultural ties.

Many incoming French *colons,* administrators, and technicians opposed the policies of Lyautey. They regarded the Moroccans as a backward, conquered people and acted according to the principle "To the victor belongs the spoils." In a report to the French government in 1920, Lyautey warned of the consequences that would follow adoption of the settlers' program. He noted that administrators and clerks coming from France and military officers coming from Algeria seemed "to have direct administration in their blood." Because of the Moroccans' different mentality and habits of living, Lyautey said, "nearly all French administrators tend more or less to regard the Moroccans as an inferior race."

The resignation—some may recall—of the aging Lyautey in 1925 brought about an intensification of this policy of "direct administration." According to the Treaty of Fez, which governed every aspect of the French presence in Morocco, France was simply to institute reforms in the Sultan's government. In practice she set up a parallel government of French administrators leaving the Moroccans purely nominal control. The Resident General dictated the choice of Sultans, and the French Secretary-General effectively superseded the Moroccan equivalent of a prime minister. The authority of the Sultan's representatives at the regional and local level (governors, pashas, and caids) was actually exercised by and through the French *Chefs des Régions* and *Contrôleurs Civils.*

The European population, which had grown from several thousand to over 350,000 demanded and received a disproportionate share of Morocco's newly exploited wealth. Families of about five thousand *colons* settled on the richest sixth of the cultivatable land, while over a million Moroccan farm families shared the rest. French skilled labor, technicians, and engineers filled all but the lowest jobs in the French-created commercial, mining, and industrial enterprises.

One French lawyer-writer, Paul Buttin, who has lived

in Morocco since 1920 discussed the attitude of many of these Europeans in his book, *Le Drame du Maroc:*

> One of their principal faults lies in equating their own interests with those of Morocco and France. They live in Morocco as if they owned it, as though it were a part of France. They know next to nothing about the history and individual personality of the country. They know Moroccans only as domestic servants, office clerks, and manual laborers, and then imagine themselves to possess an intimate knowledge of the Moroccan mentality.

Other Frenchmen, however, inspired by the dreams of Marshal Lyautey and Father Charles de Foucauld, worked to educate Moroccans for the day they would take over their own country. Dedicated teachers, doctors, agricultural specialists, and army officers opened up the twentieth century world of technology and science for new generations of Moroccans. The nucleus of an intellectual elite was formed, imbued with the traditional French ideals of liberty, equality, and brotherhood. In the 1920 report of Lyautey quoted above, he had warned that unless the authorities encouraged this elite to become leaders *with* the French, they would become leaders anyway, opposed to the French. When colonial-minded Frenchmen ignored the talents of this new class of educated Moroccans, Lyautey's prediction came true and Morocco's independence movement was born.

As had happened many times before in Morocco's history, Islam became the rallying point of opposition to foreign domination. Many of the country's greatest dynasties came to power as restorers or defenders of orthodox Islam. In 1930, the young nationalists seized on a governmental edict known as the "Berber *Dahir.*" This law, prepared by the French and dutifully signed by the twenty-year-old Mohammed V, removed the Berber population of Morocco from the jurisdiction of the Shari'a, the Islamic law regulating the lives of believing Moslems. The *dahir* also gave judicial competence to certain Berber tribal councils and even put matters of a penal nature involving Berbers under the French code of justice before reserved exclusively for non-Moslems.

Considering the religious and social importance of Islamic law, this measure not only struck at the sovereign power of the Sultan, but also at the very Islamic structure of Morocco. The young Moroccan intellectuals rallied to the defense of Islam. Supported by groups formed throughout the Moslem world, these Moroccans claimed the "Berber *Dahir*" was a move by "the eldest daughter of the Church to force millions of Moslems to embrace the Christian religion." (It was this suspicion that accounted for the attitude in 1952 of many Moroccans toward Toumliline. They simply assumed that the monks' coming to Toumliline in the very heart of Morocco's Berber-speaking country was part of this Franco-Christian policy.) In actual fact, the *dahir* was but another political move by the protectorate. Using the age-old technique of "divide and rule," they were playing on ancient differences between the rural tribes who were more casual in their practice of Islam than the Arabic-speaking more Islamicized townspeople.

The French directed the Sultan to reassure his people that the purpose of the *dahir* was not the Christianization of the Berbers. However, the *oulema* (religious scholars) of Fez, traditional interpreters of Islam in Morocco, ordered special prayers reserved only for times of peril to be recited in the mosques. In Fez crowds gathered at the holy shrine of Moulay Idriss, first Moslem King of Morocco, asking God not to separate them from their Berber brethren.

Following this, the young intellectuals formed a group which they called *Moroccan Action*. By 1934 they had drawn up a "Plan for Moroccan Reforms" which demanded that France live up to the Treaty of Fez by abolishing all traces of direct French rule and granting equality of opportunity and treatment for Moroccans in the government.

The growing strength of the nationalists concerned the Residency which forced the Sultan to outlaw the *Moroccan Action* in 1937. One of the nationalists, Allal el Fassi, a spellbinding preacher of a twentieth century Islamic Renaissance, promptly organized *The National Party for the Triumph of Reforms* and issued a call for the faithful to defend Islam. The Residency countered by exiling Allal el Fassi to French Equatorial Africa for nine years.

The outbreak of World War II and the defeat of France raised the hopes of the otherwise subdued nationalists for eventual independence. The landing of American troops in 1942 and a Casablanca conversation between Sultan Mohammed V and President Roosevelt during which the American Chief Executive spoke of ending French colonial exploitation in Morocco caused nationalist hopes to soar even higher. However, when the new Gaullist officials in the protectorate proved every bit as intransigent to nationalist demands as their Vichyite predecessors, the nationalists formed a new party called, significantly, the *Istiqlal* or Independence party. In January 1944, they fired off a manifesto demanding independence for Morocco. The Resident General replied by repeating General de Gaulle's affirmation that Morocco was "indissolubly united" to France, and imprisoned *Istiqlal* supporters and exiled its leaders.

Support for the nationalists now came from an unexpected source, Sultan Mohammed V. The French had passed over his two elder brothers and chosen him in 1927 precisely because of his youth. Gradually, however, the young Sultan became aware of his political power as the legitimate sovereign. In a speech given April, 1947, the Sultan defied the Resident General and proclaimed to the world "Morocco's ardent desire to acquire her full rights." From that moment his days as Sultan were numbered.

Within a month Morocco had a new Resident General, "a man of strength," General Alphonse Juin. This successful soldier, born in Algeria and married to the daughter of a wealthy *colon,* called for a show of French strength. He served notice on the Moroccans that he was coming "to re-establish order . . . with energetic measures." The Sultan fought back by refusing to sign any of the *dahirs* prepared by Juin, effectively nullifying the machinery of Moroccan government. As an added touch, the Sultan never shaved on days he received the Resident General.

The infuriated Juin planned with El Glaoui, the Pasha of

Toumliline

Dom Denis Martin, Prior of Toumliline

Dom Placide Pernot presents volley-ball trophy a
1957 *Cours*

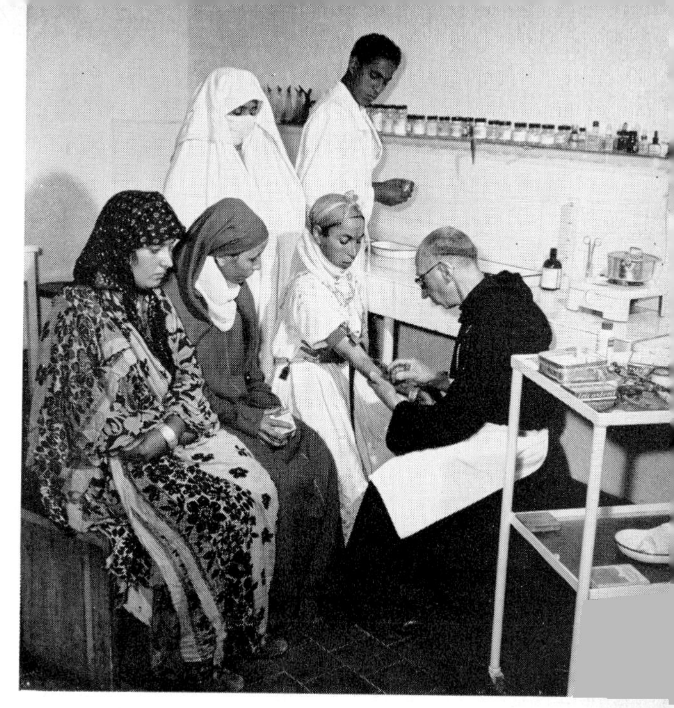

Dom Charles Lyonnet takes blood sample from tattooed Berber woman

Mme Edmund Barbaro mends socks of monks

Père Albert Peyriguère, Hermit of El-Kbab and disciple of Charles de Foucauld

Mehdi Ben Barka and Dom Denis converse at Toumliline

Ali has been at Toumliline since the death of his father in 1957

Architect Jean-Michel (in hood) confers with Marie-Antoine in workshop

Berber chief greets Crown Prince Moulay Hassan at Toumliline

Dom Jacques de Charry strings wire at monastery

Berber tribe fetes Toumliline visitors under black tents

Outdoor Community Mass at Toumliline

Marrakech and French-created lord of a million Atlas Berbers, to discredit the Sultan as compromised by "the atheistic and Communist" *Istiqlal.* The Resident-controlled Moroccan press represented El Glaoui as spokesman for millions of devout Berber Moslems who were outraged at their spiritual leader's dealings with the "atheistic nationalists." General Juin openly encouraged El Glaoui's verbal attacks on the Sultan whose "respect and traditional prestige" the Resident had sworn to protect. Then in 1951, using a carefully staged march of thousands of Berber horsemen on Rabat as a pretext, Juin imperiously commanded the Sultan to sign certain *dahirs* into law. These decrees contained provisions which would in effect give France co-sovereignty with the Sultan. The alternative was abdication.

What followed was indicative of the extent to which the central Parisian government had lost control of French policy in Morocco. Juin's ultimatum upset Paris. Foreign Minister Schuman's party newspaper condemned Juin's action and was promptly banned in Morocco. Schuman himself, in an official declaration, defended the Sultan and ruled out any talk of abdication. The Resident General, however, went right ahead with his plans, confident that the powerful North African lobby in Paris could pressure any coalition government into inaction, if not submission. With El Glaoui's Berber horsemen surrounding Rabat and French tanks ringing his palace, the Sultan capitulated to Juin's demands "to avoid bloodshed."

The repercussions in Morocco and the Islamic world to this humiliation of a Moslem monarch were immediate.

Moslem delegates to the United Nations had the Moroccan question put on the agenda of the General Assembly. The Moroccan French press nervously reported that "groups of natives are assembling silently in certain (Berber) localities where they stand for hours near the offices of the civil authorities." An anxious Paris government promoted General Juin to the post of commander in chief of NATO forces in Europe. To avoid any interpretation of this move as a sign of French weakness, Juin's supporters were able to delay his departure for six months.

The new Resident General, General Augustin Guillaume, wasted no time in letting the nationalists know exactly where he stood. In blunt terms he warned them that "rough fighting is my business," and he promised to make them "eat dirt." Tension between the nationalists and the French authorities mounted steadily during the very time preparations were being made at En-Calcat for the monks' coming to Toumliline.

After the 1952 Casablanca show of French force actually increased rather than decreased nationalist strength, French extremists decided to finish the job begun by Juin and hatched a new version of the old plan to oust the Sultan. Steps were taken to prepare world opinion which had reacted unfavorably to Juin's 1951 ultimatum causing the earlier plot to misfire. For example, in various American publications the Sultan was portrayed as a wily Oriental potentate luxuriating amidst hordes of concubines; as a medieval despot steadfastly blocking French-sponsored reforms; as a crypto-Communist ready to hand over to the Reds the $500 million string of United States strategic air bases in Morocco; as a backsliding religious leader whose antics had shocked and outraged his devout subjects.

Father Martin's French tutors concentrated on the picture of the Sultan as an oriental despot blocking democratic reforms. As one of them said:

> By the Treaty of Fez we undertook the protectorate to make Morocco into a modern state. But there exists an almost irreducible incompatibility between those terms of the Treaty which call for us to introduce reforms and those terms which guarantee the Sultan his traditional prerogatives. The principal and only real obstacle to progress in Morocco is the Sultan, or what comes to the same thing, his theocratic rule. Therefore, we must weaken and then destroy his political authority.

The Prior listened to this and similar lessons as a student would, asking questions but reserving judgment. He learned that the democratic reforms sponsored by the French authorities included plans for the election of municipal councils where both French and Moroccans could jointly control local affairs. The governmental *dahir* authorizing these elections was strenuously opposed by the Sultan whose signature was necessary for it to become law.

However, the Prior's Moroccan tutor, Si Bekkai, had an explanation for this. Not only would the election of joint French-Moroccan municipal councils give the 350,000 French equal representation with over 9,000,000 Moroccans, he told Father Martin, but worse still, it would seriously compromise if not destroy the sovereignty of Morocco. Under the Treaty of Fez the French in Morocco had absolutely no political rights. They were visitors only, not citizens. Should the Sultan sign the *dahir*, Si Bekkai explained, he would sign away the existence of a sovereign Morocco and the country would become, like Algeria, a colony of France. The Sultan sincerely desired political reforms, Si Bekkai assured the prior. In his 1950 annual speech from the Throne, Mohammed V had insisted that "not for a single moment have we lost sight of the fact that the best regime under which a sovereign and self-administered country can live is the democratic, such as we know it in the world today."

Father Martin enjoyed Si Bekkai's visits. This former lieutenant colonel in the French cavalry who had lost a leg in the Ardennes retained his military bearing. He came dressed always in an immaculate white *djellaba* (a flowing, ankle length hooded robe), white heelless leather slippers, and a red fez. On his very first visit to Toumliline, Father Martin called a special chapter for his monks to meet the Pasha. In the refectory, Si Bekkai was given the place of honor at the right hand of the prior, a spot usually reserved for visiting abbots and bishops. In turn, when Father Martin visited the Pasha in Sefrou, he was installed on the cushion of honor and proffered the choicest portions of meat.

Although his French and Moroccan sources pictured the political situation in contradictory terms, Dom Denis could not doubt, with but one or two exceptions, the complete sincerity of his friends. "I learned a very important lesson from this," he recalls, "because I saw how it was possible for good people, sincerely religious people, to have a distorted view on things because of certain military or political preoccupations."

In working his way through the maze of Moroccan politics, the prior went often to see the Vicar Apostolic, Archbishop Lefèvre. This gentle Franciscan, with the benevolent, paternal face, gave him much sound advice. He had given similar counsel to his diocesan priests in an explosive pastoral letter, dated February 15, 1952. In that letter he detailed the obligations imposed on Christians living in Morocco and outlined the conditions justifying their presence there. Stressing their status as guests, he called for sincere attempts to get to know their hosts. He cautioned Morocco's Christians, many of whom were employers, to be particularly attentive to the demands of social justice. Referring to the political tempest, he told his priests, "now, more than ever, the ideals of justice and charity must be ours. We have not the right to be partisans. We must never forget that we are called to be the witnesses of Christ and to love *all* our brothers. The Christian must seek out and love justice, wherever it manifests itself. Nothing is more difficult, in times of crisis, than this objectivity and this serenity. That is why we must pray much and, in the midst of agitation, remain docile to the Holy Spirit."

The Prior's greatest source of information about the Moroccan scene, as might be expected, were the Moroccans themselves whom he came to know and respect. One young man, a son of a leading Moroccan theologian, spoke to Father Martin of a crisis facing the younger generation.

"I wonder [he said] if you realize just how uncomfortable the situation of a young Moroccan is. Take me, for example. I have a French baccalaureate plus a degree in French law. My father is a very cultured man, a scholar, but knows only things Arabic. In our house only Arabic may be spoken, not a word of French. This means that I am no longer able to feel at home in my own house. At the same time, I am no more at home in a completely French atmosphere. All this has happened to me as a result of what I have learned in your French schools.

"Paradoxically [he continued] those same schools have given me a most vivid sense of being a Moroccan, of belonging to a country. I love my country very much and feel personally humiliated when I see my country ground down under French control. All the reasons I have for violently opposing the French regime in Morocco have been taught me by the French. Yet, I will always be marked by my formation in French culture. I cannot return to the ways of my father."

In a Moslem country, this cultural crisis could not help but involve a religious crisis as well. The young Moslems had a religion which developed historically along with a complex of institutions and customs difficult to integrate with a modern Western secular civilization. What could they do? One might follow the example of some of the older generation, who expressed their fidelity to Islam by simply refusing to live in the political and social twentieth century. Or, remaining true to Islam, one might follow the nationalist hero, Allal al Fassi, and work for an Islamic renaissance. Still another possibility was to ape the secular aspects of the modern West, keeping only the appearances of Islam demanded by the Moslem community. A more extreme step would be to embrace the atheism consonant with a Marxist view of the world. But however the Moroccan youth were to resolve their cultural and religious schizophrenia, one thing was apparent to Father Martin: their support of the nationalist movement against the French regime was total.

After six months of acquiring an intensive political education, Father Martin could appreciate the suspicions of Toumliline's Moslem neighbors. Against the background of the "Berber *Dahir*," the coming of French monks to the very Berber town where the French had located their special Berber college would seem to be but another move in the protectorate's *politique Berbère.* And although at their inaugural ceremonies Abbot Dom Marie de Floris had told French officials of Toumliline's determination to be independent of the military, and though this had been the purpose of the Prior's not so gentle declaration on the same subject to the local *commandant,* Colonel Clesca, Father Martin understood that the Moroccans still identified the monastery with the French military.

CHAPTER 7

"I UNDERSTAND you monks are mixing in politics," Colonel Clesca said to Dom Gilbert, whom he had stopped on a street in Azrou. It was the first week of July, 1953.

The monk, cellarer of Toumliline, fought to keep his temper in hand as he asked the officer what he was talking about.

"You know exactly what I mean, Father. You monks have been giving tea to the political prisoners working on the aqueduct in front of the monastery."

"One of them came to us for water . . ."

". . . and you gave them tea. Who told you to?"

"The Prior. He said to treat them as guests."

"Guests! Why do you think I have a guard around them!"

"Oh, but we gave tea to the soldiers, too." The monk smiled just enough to infuriate Clesca.

"One cup of tea, one *spoonful* of tea given to *one* of my prisoners is mixing in politics, the kind of mixing that hurts us!"

When Dom Denis learned of the conversation, he smiled at the cellarer and said, "I'm very angry at you, Father."

Gilbert realized, smile or no smile, that he was being reprimanded. "You should know I don't want you to get into street corner debates. Don't do it again." Dismissing the monk, he asked that he send the sub-Prior to him.

The Prior explained, when Father Jean-Marie appeared, that the two of them were going to visit Clesca. He wanted the sub-Prior along to take notes.

"But before we go see that the prisoners are given tea. This may be the last time they get any from us."

Father Jean-Marie decided to make the tea himself. He went through the refectory and into the kitchen, gathered together a number of small pots, filled them with water, then placed them on top of the cast-iron coal stove that ran the length of one wall. He followed this by rounding up the ingredients he needed: green Chinese tea, two five-pound cones of sugar, and the basket of mint bought by Father Gilbert that morning in Azrou. While the water heated on the stove, he took a huge pot from the wall, covered the bottom with tea and overlaid it with a springy bed of mint. Then he hammered the cones of sugar into small chunks and put these on top of the mint. Finally when the water boiled, he poured it into the pot.

With Ali, the monastery cook, trailing behind carrying a basket of cups, the sub-Prior hauled the steaming pot the eighty yards from the kitchen to the road. The first cup of tea he gave to the chief of the Berber guards, Moulay Ismail, a bearded giant of six-foot-five, formidable with his white cotton uniform, red cartridge belt and sub-machine gun.

The thirty prisoners put down their tools and gathered

around the monk and Moulay Ismail. "You're early today," one of them said.

"We see Clesca in a little while," the priest explained.

"Say hello for me," someone shouted. The group laughed, Moulay Ismail, the loudest. He waved in the eight other guards and told them to have some tea.

The prisoners had been working in front of the monastery for a week digging a ditch for pipes that were to run water to Azrou from the spring of Toumliline half a mile above the monastery. Ostensibly they had all been arrested because they had signed a telegram to the President of the French Republic objecting to pressure exerted on the Sultan by two hundred and seventy French-appointed pashas and caids. The real reason for their roundup—the total had included more than a hundred in Azrou—was that Clesca had discovered the list of local cell leaders of the *Istiqlal,* outlawed the previous December.

Looking around him at the smiling crowd of prisoners, Father Jean-Marie was once again amazed at the ability of Moroccans to live for the moment. They were enjoying the tea, the national antidote against the African sun, and this gesture of concern by the monks. But he knew from their blistered hands that they had had little experience with manual labor. They were teachers and merchants; one was even a hairdresser. The sub-Prior thought of the stories told him by Brother Marie-Antoine of his five years as a German slave laborer and wondered if these men faced the same hell.

The priest left Ali in charge and he headed for the

Prior's office. Dom Denis asked "Ready?" and the monk nodded.

As they walked to the Peugeot 203, Dom Denis saw Father Gilbert patiently teaching Benedictine sign language to a deaf-mute Moroccan boy just come to the monastery. Without breaking stride, he tapped Gilbert on the back of the head and said, "I'm still angry."

A captain showed the two monks into Colonel Clesca's office. The officer stood up and offered his hand to both men.

"I was about to leave for the monastery," he told the Prior.

"Why?"

"I was just informed you gave tea to my prisoners again today." At this point, Dom Marie took out a small notebook and a pen and sat down. Clesca, knowing the meeting was going to be a showdown, wondered if he should call in his aide to take notes, too.

The Colonel looked the part he played: the tough military-civil boss of an area verging on revolution. He was tall and square built, and, for a man of sixty, in remarkably good shape. His eyes were black, his beard was black, and his eyeglasses were framed with heavy black horn. His bald head was as square as his body. Clesca, Dom Denis knew, was much more than the usual run of professional soldier—he was intelligent, imaginative. He had been told about this man who was his own best intelligence officer, that he knew everyone around Azrou—merchants, teachers, students, Berbers who came out of the hills to buy and sell on *souk* day.

The Prior knew, too, he had not gone as far as he might have, because in a class-conscious French army the Colonel was only the son of a school teacher and was married to the daughter of a Beaune lawyer. Dom Denis judged he just wanted to do his job as well as he could until he retired.

On the other hand, the Colonel knew next to nothing about Dom Denis. He recalled only the Prior's naive refusal to have anything to do with French military in the event of an uprising and decided he would be harsh on the man.

Dom Denis, though, didn't give the Colonel a chance to direct the conversation. "I understand you accuse us of mixing in politics."

Clesca, taken off guard, answered, "I never said that."

"That's what Father Gilbert told me and I believe what he said."

"I did complain about your giving tea to my prisoners . . ."

". . . and you said that was mixing in politics."

"I don't remember using the phrase."

"It's not what you said that bothers me. What bothers me is that you said it to Father Gilbert. I told you once before that I'm responsible for what goes on at the monastery. I don't want you to deal with me through intermediaries. I demand that you deal with me directly. I say this to you because I know you like frankness. It's what I like, too."

"Of course I prefer to be frank. Now tell me, why do you give tea to my prisoners?"

"They were thirsty."

Clesca's hand pounded the arm of his chair as he said, "Don't be naive, Father."

"Is it naive to give tea to men who are thirsty?"

"If they're political prisoners of the French and you're a Frenchman, yes, it's naive." The officer almost shouted: "Do you realize the importance of what you've done? I arrested those men because I got my hands on the list of men who head the *Istiqlal* around here. I had to arrest them. Many of them were men that I knew. And what do you do! You give them tea. You proclaim to the world that what I've done is unjust."

"What I did I did out of Christian charity and not because of politics."

"But, Father, Christian charity doesn't preclude prudence."

"Every man I meet that needs help will get help."

"You're wrong on that point, Father. Those prisoners don't need help. They're not suffering. I'm afraid you've been misled by Peyriguère. He's constantly chattering about French injustices in Morocco."

"We're not talking about Father Peyriguère. We're talking about your prisoners."

"Well, they're *not* mistreated. I plan to pass judgment the day after tomorrow. They'll be back home in a few months."

"All of them?"

"Of course not. The more guilty ones will be sent to prison in Meknes for two years. What does it matter? You've seen for yourself that they're not badly off. Oh, of course, the police may have been guilty of some brutality toward them. This I don't know. The police always have their customs. This is inevitable."

"It seems to me a prisoner, no matter how he's treated, is bound to be unhappy because he's lost his liberty."

"You're still new in Morocco, Father. The prisoners are being fed and housed for nothing. They're happy."

"How can they be when they're cut off from their families."

Clesca suddenly lost track of the conversation and half-muttered, "Their families?" He slapped the arm of his chair again. "Their families! Now that we bring up the subject, will you tell me why the families of the prisoners walk to the monastery every day?"

"They come to cook for the men."

"You *are* naive, Father. By now there isn't a Moroccan within a hundred miles of Azrou that doesn't know what you've done."

"A man shouldn't be separated from his wife and children."

"If you only knew how Moroccans treated their wives and how they changed them so easily. My wife has several women working for her who were sent away by their husbands. All a man has to do is to say 'I divorce you' three times and the women are homeless." The Colonel walked to one of the windows in his office and looked out at the manicured lawn. "Prisoners are not unhappy with us. I always have gardeners who are in custody. After we tell them they are released, they always ask to stay."

The Colonel turned around and looked at Dom Denis.

"Father, I insist that you have no contact with my prisoners in the future. I want you to understand that."

"Every time I see someone suffering, I will help. And if I do this, I will not be mixing in politics, I'll simply be doing my duty as a Christian."

"All right, we understand each other," Clesca said resignedly. "I'll take the prisoners some place else so that they can't have contact with you. I tell you, Father, these men can't distinguish between a charitable act and a political one."

"That's not my impression. You know yourself Moslems are taught they must give alms to the poor. Furthermore, they know us as *marabouts*, as men of prayer."

"Nonetheless, you're damaging my position. Personally, as a Christian, I understand your attitude. But on the political plane, I disapprove."

"I disagree. I don't think what we do contradicts what you do. We represent France as fully as you do. I think our presence contributes to friendship between France and Morocco. I believe this is true whether we give tea to your prisoners or receive, as we do, children from Azrou at our monastery."

"I've heard of those children. I know that you even have some working at the monastery. I assume you're aware we arrested one of them the other day. He had broken into the kiosk in Azrou and stolen some French books."

The Prior smiled as he exclaimed, "This proves his interest in literature."

"They were cheap novels."

"He has not yet developed discernment."

"It will be good by the time he returns."

"I'm sure he'll appreciate his education."

"I warn you, Father, that you must not proselytize the youngsters who go to your monastery. The law forbids it. And even if it didn't, the people here would kill you as soon as they found out about it."

"Don't you know that all priests in Morocco are forbidden to proselytize by the Church? We bear testimony to Christ and nothing more."

Clesca decided to bring up another subject. "Why is it that you have your French students waiting on tables when you have Moroccans in the refectory?"

"It's good for them. They do it enthusiastically, too."

"Have any of the parents complained?"

"None. In fact some have written congratulating us on promoting friendship between Moroccans and the French."

"Make sure you don't promote this friendship by giving any more tea to the prisoners. Understand me: I forbid it."

"I've already told you that I will help any man who needs help."

"You realize that if you interfere again, you might be deported back to France—all of you monks."

"It's all the same to me."

The Prior stood up and told the silent Father Jean-Marie it was time to go. Turning once again to the Colonel, he said, "I'm sure you prefer this frankness to maneuvers on my part. And from now on, if there are differences between us, we will talk directly and not through intermediaries. Is that agreed?"

"Agreed."

The car was halfway to Toumliline before Father Jean-Marie asked, "Is this the end of the business?"

The Prior pretended shock as he mimicked Clesca: "Don't be naive, Father."

Back in his office, Clesca began to write a report to his superior, General Roger Miquel, Chief of the Meknes Region. He would state the facts and nothing more to his superior: the Prior was a tough one and he liked him.

On August tenth Dom Denis found a note on his desk from the sub-Prior saying that an army officer, who wanted to remain anonymous, had come to warn the Prior. The note read:

> At the last meeting of the general staff in Meknes, General Miquel told of a report from Military Security in Paris that stated the Father Abbot of Toumliline had adopted the political ideas of Father Peyriguère and was speaking against the Residence and against France. The report referred particularly to an unnamed monk of Toumliline who had attacked France in two different houses in Azrou. The general said: "If this is true, I will close the abbey in twenty-four hours." The official also warned we must be cautious about *every* visitor at Toumliline. They might come just to make trouble for the monastery. He also says that in Azrou there is a secret policeman charged with watching Toumliline.

After rereading the note, Dom Denis carefully scratched out the name of the officer who had spoken to Father Jean-Marie.

That night in Chapter, Martin reviewed the Clesca interview with the community and told his monks of the warning he had received. He thought it possible, he said, that Miquel himself had sent the informant to scare them. Then he said, "Did any of you make a political statement in Azrou about France?"

One monk suggested this charge might stem from a happening at the sanatorium a month ago. Père Peyriguère had been invited to speak to the patients there by Père Placide, he reminded the Prior, and maybe it was Peyriguère who had spoken against France. All agreed, however, it was nothing said by anyone in the community.

Four days later Martin wrote to General Miquel. He said he had heard Toumliline was accused by the Military Security in Paris of attacking France and the residency and quoted Miquel as having said, "If this is true, I will close the abbey in twenty-four hours." Fearing summary expulsion, he said, he had gone to Rabat and told Archbishop Lefèvre about the accusation against Toumliline, and then with Lefèvre's permission, protested at the residency against the possibility of Miquel acting on the basis of an unverified report. Dom Denis demanded to see the general in order to find out the precise accusations brought against Toumliline. "If these accusations are found to be baseless, the General must tell each officer who had been at the meeting at which Toumliline had been attacked of the truth."

It was a strong letter; so strong in fact that Martin decided against mailing it. Instead, he drove to Meknes to see Miquel. Father Jean-Marie was again in tow.

As soon as they were led into the general's office, Martin said: "Somebody has told us you are angry at Toumliline."

The general sat down at his desk after greeting the two monks. "Angry? This is a strong word. To be exact, I have been disturbed about you."

Dom Denis ignored the remark. "It's been reported to me that you told several of your officers we have attacked France and the residency."

The general, exuding charm, smiled at the furious monk. "Those are grave charges, Father, and if I had had to formulate them, I would have been pained. Moreover, I would have spoken to you before this. But no, the report you heard is not true. I have been troubled, however, because I fear that Father Peyriguère has had a bad influence on you." The general's dark eyes never left the monk's face as he talked.

The thought occurred again to Dom Denis that Miquel might have engineered this confrontation by sending the informant to him. First the report of Miquel's fury at Toumliline, then the emphatic disclaimer, and finally the gentle hint that he should not associate with Peyriguère—it was a classic police procedure for frightening a suspect and putting him on his good behavior. But then again the residency, after the Prior had made his protest, could have told the general that, report or no report from Military Security, he was to leave the monastery alone. In any event, Dom Denis knew he had to keep his anger in check, for if Miquel was his enemy he would try to destroy him with his own words.

Remaining calm was a problem for the Prior. He instinctively distrusted the general and disliked him, suspecting that at the very least he was trying to play him off against Peyriguère. Everything about the towering officer set him off. He sat in his chair, Dom Denis thought, as if he were posing for his portrait: casual, self-assured, his chest thrust out, his underslung jaw, permanently dark because of a heavy beard, jutting forward. Even the swagger stick that the general was toying with annoyed the monk.

"The subject of Father Peyriguère," the Prior said angrily, "has nothing to do with why I am here. Let me repeat that I have been told you received a report from Paris accusing us of attacking France and the residency. *Is this true?*"

"It is absolutely false. I've received nothing from Paris about you. But there is an incident in March that occurred at the sanatorium that disturbs me."

"Yes, yes, I know. But we weren't involved."

"Just as I thought. But I did hear that Peyriguère had gone there at the invitation of one of your monks."

"Not exactly. Père Placide is a monk of En-Calcat, he is not a member of our community. But tell me what Père Peyriguère supposedly said."

"He said that if he were a Moroccan he would not like the French."

"The sentence has been taken out of context. He was speaking to a French audience and mentioned that he often travels wearing a *djellaba.* And when he does this, he is always mistaken for a Berber. He said that Frenchmen, when they see him, back away because they think contact with him would give them lice. And what he told his audience was that if he were in fact a Moroccan he would hate the French for this."

The general exclaimed, "That is exactly the same phrase!"

"Not quite. It is even worse than the one you heard. Peyriguère had said, 'If I were a Moroccan, I would hate the French.' But please remember he was talking to a French audience and that he was referring to the Frenchman's contempt for Moroccans."

"You don't know the man! In Ifrane recently he had the effrontery to preach an *incendiary* sermon against what he calls injustices in Morocco. And I was in the church!"

"Incredible," the Prior said as he smiled for the first time.

"*Nothing* stops him. He writes to Paris, to the Resident General, to the newspapers, to the Archbishop. I decided I had to put a stop to it so I complained to the Archbishop about him and suggested it would be better if he sent Peyriguère back to France. And do you know what happened? The Archbishop told Peyriguère of my complaint and a few days later I received a violent, nasty letter from him. Of course, I did not answer. I forwarded the letter to the proper authorities."

"General, we know very well that Peyriguère has strong opinions about the protectorate, but they do not influence us. He comes to Toumliline to rest and work. The Archbishop has asked us to receive him. Moreover, he is valuable to us because he knows the Berbers better than any Frenchman in the country."

"That is true."

"But as for the accusation that we speak against France, it should be easy for you to establish the truth or falsity of this. Speak to our friends. Ask Archbishop Lefèvre. Ask Colonel de Tournemire."

"Ah, Colonel de Tournemire. I have heard a report that he has 'evolved' and that he now shares the ideas of François Mauriac."

"What do you base this on?"

"A report. In Morocco, my friend, one must be extremely cautious about everything one says. The smallest word is held up to scrutiny."

"Then you of course know about my differences with Colonel Clesca."

"Yes. He has written me about the tea incident. But don't judge him harshly. He is naturally a blunt man."

"I don't mind his bluntness. But as I told him, he and I must be frank with one another. I demanded that he not deal through an intermediary with me as he did the other day when he complained to my cellarer, Father Gilbert. I told him that I am the superior and that I alone am responsible."

"You were right to tell him that."

"Do you also agree I was justified in giving the political prisoners tea?"

"You were quite right in doing that."

"You approve?"

"Yes, just so long as there was no conversation between the monks and the political prisoners. This is forbidden. Did you speak to them?"

The Prior decided to side-step the question. "Colonel

Clesca said the *giving* of tea was political. You understand we cannot renounce our mission. We are witnesses of Christ and of the Church. If Moroccans cannot distinguish between a political act and a charitable act, then we must teach them. We must begin now."

"Your position is very strong," the General agreed. "It is unassailable."

"Then I may continue to do what I've been doing?"

"If I were in your place, I would do the same thing."

"And you do not object that we receive young Berbers at the monastery?"

"Oh, I approve absolutely. But don't make the mistake of trusting their word too much, nor of counting on them. They are capable of anything. You will be disappointed."

"But we cannot be disappointed because we expect nothing. We are here as witnesses. We are here to give testimony to the charity of Christ."

"This is very beautiful. Then you are the only ones who will never be disappointed."

"General, I see that you approve of what we're doing and I won't detain you any longer."

"I approve of the tea. I also think that you ought to receive at your monastery any one you wish."

"And in the future if there are any misunderstandings between us, we will deal directly with one another."

"Yes. If I have anything to say to you, I will either call or come see you."

"Good. Intermediaries distort so easily."

"This is not the first time I've had to clear up a misunderstanding with a priest. And oddly enough they always come around to the same point. They all ask the right to proselytize and baptize."

"We don't ask for that. We only ask for the right to bear witness."

"That is what Charles de Foucauld wanted. That is what Peyriguère says he wants, but because of his immense pride will never be able to do. Peyriguère wears the habit of De Foucauld, he claims to be his successor, but he does not accomplish the same thing, nor can he. De Foucauld had a formation. *He was an aristocrat. He was an officer.*"

CHAPTER 8

THE tea incident, "a simple act of charity" as Dom Denis called it, had many effects. The most immediate was that it satisfied their Moroccan neighbors that the monks were not, as they had suspected, French agents. But much more than this, the episode catapulted the monastery into the middle of Moroccan history.

Three days after the prior's conversation with General Miquel, the French succeeded in their plot to depose Mohammed V, a plot that had aborted in 1951. This time the Pasha of Marrakech, El Glaoui, appeared with a petition demanding the Sultan's abdication. It was signed by nearly all of Morocco's French-appointed pashas and caids. (Among the handful of nonsigners was the Pasha of Sefrou, Father Martin's friend, Si Bekkai.) Once again lightly armed Berber horsemen "spontaneously" marched on Rabat and reduced the French force of tanks, machine-guns and jet planes to a state of self-proclaimed helplessness. The only way the French residency could honor its obligation to protect the Sultan, it said, was to *fly* him *out* of the country. Clad in pajamas, Mohammed V was whisked first to Corsica and then to Madagascar. His exile had begun.

Unlike 1951, when General Juin gave Paris advance notice, the 1953 *coup d'état* was presented as a *fait accompli* to Premier Laniel. Laniel did nothing to protest the maneuver. However, there was violent reaction in France to the development. It was led by Nobel prize winner François Mauriac and a group of Catholic intellectuals, among them the journalist Robert Barrat. Since their exposé of the real causes of the bloody Casablanca riots, these men had tried to awaken France to what they termed her dishonor at the hands of the *colons* in Morocco. Mauriac became a household word in Morocco because of his denunciation of Guillaume. More than ever, he was revered by Moroccans, reviled by *colons*.

Organized counteraction against the Sultan's deposition was cut short in Morocco by the roundup of several thousand *Istiqlal* supporters who were shipped without trial to join their leaders in large detention camps on the edge of the Sahara. Gradually, however, the Moroccan people united around the symbol of their exiled spiritual leader, even deserting their mosques where prayers were ordered said in the name of the French puppet, Mohammed VI. Younger, more radical nationalists replaced the imprisoned moderates as leaders of Moroccan resistance and began a campaign of terror. The disemboweled bodies of Moroccan collaborators were found almost daily. French factories, farms, and crops were set afire, cafés and trains were bombed. Father Martin's cousin, General Marie-Antoine d'Hauteville, was among the French officers wounded by terrorist bullets.

The Residency retaliated once again with mass arrests, curfews, and "interrogations" that often took the lives of those questioned. American readers were given an eye-witness report by *Time* correspondent Frank White of one French *rattisage* or roundup. He told of French troops surrounding a native quarter, dragging out every male except small boys, then forcing them to run one by one between parallel lines of troops who clubbed them with rifle butts. The Civil Controller in charge of the operation, a French veteran of thirty-three years in Morocco, apologized to the correspondent, White reported. "We know these people," he said, "and to do anything less would be to invite further disturbances." White added a laconic note: "In the course of the roundup twenty Arabs died." In an effort to relieve tensions, Paris replaced Resident General Guillaume in May, 1954, with a civilian, Francis Lacoste.

During this first year of the Sultan's exile and the consequent terrorist activity, the atmosphere around Toumliline was relatively calm. A French Army report on political conditions in the area commented:

> One cannot pass over in silence the influence which the Benedictine fathers have in certain areas. Their presence at Toumliline attracts to the monastery numerous French, Moroccan and foreign visitors, some official, some not. . . . (The Benedictines') total ignorance of the Moroccan mentality and the situation in Morocco caused them to make mistakes at the be-

> ginning and to do some surprising things. However, their repetition now seems remote.

But with the Benedictine tradition of opening their monastery doors to all who knock, "surprising things" were never remote. One hot August morning in 1954, a new phase in the monks' relations with the Moroccans began. Brother Cyprian, the aging monastery gatekeeper, told Father Martin that Paul Buttin had just arrived. The prior hurried to the gate house. Buttin, a slim, erect French lawyer from Meknes who had spent thirty-five years in North Africa, had been a friend of Toumliline from the first days. An articulate Christian, he had for many years in books and articles attempted to define the Christian's responsibilities in North Africa. Father Martin had great respect for this man whose stand during the present crisis had cost him most of his European practice and social ostracism for his family.

There was a Moroccan with Buttin. "Dom Denis," he said, "I would like you to meet a friend and colleague of mine, Monsieur Driss M'Hammedi."

The Prior, though this was the first time he had met this dark, barrel-chested Moroccan, knew he was talking to one of the leaders of the *Istiqlal.* He was surprised to see him, since M'Hammedi had been arrested more than a year before and put into prison. Buttin, M'Hammedi's lawyer, had often mentioned the Resident General's refusal to acknowledge Buttin's demands that the Moroccan at least be given a trial. The priest's face showed confusion.

"It's all right, Father," Driss said. "I was released from custody and arrived back in Meknes yesterday."

Buttin explained that the new Resident General, Francis Lacoste—he emphasized the word "new"—had granted amnesty to many of the *Istiqlal* leaders held in Arbalou du Kerdous, a detention camp in the Moroccan Sahara.

M'Hammedi picked up the conversation at this point. "I wanted my first visit to be with you, Father. I know you are our friend."

The Prior asked why he believed this. M'Hammedi smiled and said, "Tea." He explained that at the detention camp everyone knew of the tea the monks had given to the political prisoners: the word had been spread by the prisoners who had worked near the monastery.

"It was a little thing," Dom Denis said.

"It was a little thing, yes, but significant. You showed us that real Christians rebelled at injustices in this country."

Over lunch in the Prior's office, M'Hammedi told Dom Denis he also knew about his argument with Clesca and Miquel. The report, Driss explained, had come by *téléphone arabe*—the French talk at table, the servants listen, and what is found out in Azrou one day is known in Casablanca and Rabat the next and in every part of the country within a week.

During the meal, Father Martin learned Driss M'Hammedi's background. He was from Fez, the son of a doorman and a member of the tribe Beni M'Hammedi, whence his name. He had been educated in the local Koranic school until he was 14, when his father died. His uncle then took charge of the boy and sent him to the French *lycée* in Fez. With his baccalaureate behind him, he went to Rabat to enter the government service. Working in the daytime and studying law at night, he was admitted to the bar. Driss organized a Moslem Boy Scout movement in 1937. The French authorities, however, afraid such an organization might turn into a training school for nationalists, discouraged him. Driss then suggested his organization be incorporated into the French Catholic Scouts in Morocco, but the authorities turned him down on the grounds the French scouts might attempt proselytizing. At the outbreak of World War II they suppressed the Moslem Scouts completely. Driss joined the *Istiqlal* party when it was formed in late 1943 and was sent to organize the Meknes area. Operating both as lawyer and *Istiqlal* organizer, he had great success until the roundup of top *Istiqlal* leaders after the Casablanca riots in December, 1952.

"I am free now," Driss said, "but not for long. Though the new Resident General has released some of us, I still live in Meknes under the jurisdiction of General Miquel. The general is looking for the slightest pretext to throw me into prison."

As M'Hammedi and Buttin prepared to leave after lunch, the Moroccan told Father Martin that his six-year-old son Ali had begged him not to leave the house that morning. "Don't go, Papa," Driss quoted him as saying, "you will not come home again."

Father Martin saw Driss often after this first meeting. He considered him an extremely intelligent, openhearted man. They had many discussions on religious matters. Driss' "spiritual director" was the Grand Sheik of Islam in Morocco, the *Fqih* Bel Larbi el Alaoui, who was also, in a way, "spiritual adviser" to Father Martin on things Islamic.

In Rabat on business one day, the Prior was followed into a bookshop by a French Army officer, his friend, Colonel Devillars, director of the protectorate's Political Affairs Department.

"Dom Denis, you see Driss M'Hammedi occasionally, don't you? Could you do me a favor? The Resident General released Driss and the other prisoners in the hope of arranging a reconciliation between them and those Moroccans working with our administration. He invited them to dinner. The first time, the *Istiqlal* leaders came, but apparently they found it disagreeable since they did not come to the second dinner. Now, one of the leaders we cannot reach is Driss M'Hammedi. Could you ask him to see us?"

"I'll speak to him about it, but if I do you must ask your chief, Colonel Hubert, to place him under the Residency's special protection to forestall any action by General Miquel."

"Agreed."

The next morning Father Martin went to Meknes and told Driss of his conversation. "Talk with them," he advised, "and maybe they can solve your problem with General Miquel." He telephoned Driss' acceptance to Devillars and arranged a meeting later in the day. Piling into the monastery car, they drove to Rabat and met the Colonel at his home. Father Martin was a quiet observer as the French and then the Moroccan positions were defined. The Colonel suggested that Driss move to Rabat, where he would no longer be under Miquel's thumb. Driss agreed.

A short time later Father Martin was introduced by Driss to Mehdi Ben Barka, a thirty-four-year-old mathematics professor and the youngest signer of the 1944 *Istiqlal* manifesto. The meeting took place at a reunion of the recently released prisoners. The Prior met also Mohammed el Fassi, former Rector of the ancient Karaouine University and a founder of *Istiqlal,* and Captain Mahjoubi Aherdane, a Berber nationalist who later organized the Moroccan Army of Liberation. "It was," Father Martin recalls, "a cordial, sympathetic meeting." The most important event of the evening was that Ben Barka asked the prior to visit him at his home. He accepted an invitation for the next evening.

"What can you do for us?" Ben Barka bluntly asked the priest as soon as amenities were over.

"What do you expect me to do?"

"We want independence for our country. But we feel we need the help of those who know the realities of the situation here and who are at the same time disinterested. Since 1920 and especially since 1951, Frenchmen and Moroccans have lived in worlds separated by passions and prejudices. I believe that among the French here our only hope is with certain Catholics. So I would like you to put us in touch with them."

"It's possible. But let me think about the best way to go about it."

His first step was to consult Archbishop Lefèvre who told him to go ahead. Next he spoke to close French friends. They all advised caution because of counterterrorist activities against those favoring Franco-Moroccan co-operation, pointing out that such groups as "The White Hand" and "The Anti-Terrorist Defense Organization" were now attacking and killing Frenchmen as well as Moroccans. (That July, for example, they killed three members of the family of a Casablanca attorney in separate bomb and machine gun attacks. His crime: he had assembled French and Moroccan business and professional men at his home to discuss ways of improving Franco-Moroccan relations. Even the new Resident General, Francis Lacoste, was not immune from verbal attacks. Violent tracts denouncing Lacoste's "criminal blindness' and his "policy of treason" were distributed by the tens of thousands. Singled out as particularly treasonable was Lacoste's release of Driss M'Hammedi and the other *Istiqlal* leaders, and worse still, his desire "to begin conversations with these enemies of France and Morocco.")

One friend Father Martin consulted was a wealthy *colon* who had been quite generous to Toumliline. The Prior telephoned to ask if he could bring Driss M'Hammedi along. He wanted to see for himself the reactions of both the *colon* and the nationalist in this dress rehearsal for later meetings. The Frenchman received the *Istiqlal* leader warmly. Driss sensed this acceptance and responded in kind. The *colon's* wife, however, gave Morocco's future Minister of the Interior a chilly reception. Father Martin noticed she tried hard but just could not overcome her repugnance at entertaining a "native" at her table. After the visit, the *colon* exposed himself to the double danger of terrorist and counterterrorist attack by accompanying

Driss to the *medina* (Moroccan quarter) where he was to spend the night. Driss later told the Prior that the *colon's* sensitivity to the traditions of Moroccan hospitality, where an invited guest is the host's responsibility both on the way to and from his home, put the seal on their new friendship.

Encouraged by this, Father Martin organized the first meeting with the help of Raymond Fourquez, a wealthy young *colon.* He told him of Ben Barka's request and asked if he would come to the monastery for lunch with the nationalists. Fourquez agreed and was told to bring some friends. For the lunch the Prior ordered the monastery cellarer to forget the budget and to serve the best meal possible. Fourquez with two friends and Ben Barka with two nationalists arrived within minutes of each other. Throughout lunch, the conversation was guardedly polite. Later, over the *café filtre* and mint tea, the meeting went to pieces.

The *colons* had brought up the difficulties they were having in getting co-operation from their Moroccan employees. Ben Barka calmly said, "Then you had better leave the running of our country to us. We have only to give the sign and the people will co-operate." Father Martin quickly brought the meeting to a close.

Escorting the Frenchmen to their car, the Prior listened to their complaints. "The idiots!" one *colon* said. "They haven't the faintest idea of business management, let alone government. Heaven help Morocco if they ever come to power! They think they have but to snap their fingers and the country will run itself."

Father Martin returned to lead the Moroccans to their car. This time he listened politely to their complaints. "These Frenchmen are stubborn and conceited. They think we are incapable of running our own affairs. Such superiority complexes! It is painful to deal with such people."

The second meeting was at the home of Fourquez, who had invited the important *colons* of the Rabat-Casablanca region as well as Ben Barka, who came with a number of *Istiqlal* men. It, too, produced nothing. The third meeting was at the house of Si Nejjai, a Moroccan who had come to the earlier meetings with Ben Barka. An agricultural engineer who was later to be Minister of Agriculture, he had many ideas about evolving Morocco's agricultural economy but had gotten nowhere with the French authorities. Just before the meeting, Father Martin met separately with the two groups and asked them not to sabotage the discussions. To improve the chances for an understanding, he tried to explain to each side the difficulties of the other, and begged them to avoid incendiary remarks. Partly because of this, and partly because they were beginning to know each other, the meeting began and ended cordially.

Following this, the French *colons* invited Father Martin to meet some of *their* Moroccan friends, in particular a certain Pasha. The most important Frenchmen of the region were around the lunch table. Father Martin knew of this Moroccan. The French had appointed him to office to embarrass the Sultan, Mohammed V, with whom the Moroccan had had a bitter dispute. Deeply committed to them, he was regarded by the French as a "true Moroccan" and one of their staunchest allies. In conversation with him, Dom Denis learned that the Pasha was a frightened man. He felt that the days of French control were numbered and would have liked to switch sides but was too involved to make the break. What most distressed the Prior was that his French friends were convinced that this frightened Pasha spoke for the Moroccan people. How could they possibly understand the men of *Istiqlal*? These friends of Father Martin probably thought the same as the French official who described the *Istiqlal* as "a collection of intellectuals with half-baked ideas about Western democracy and the French Revolution who have swallowed the Communist line and who are actually despised by their own people."

These meetings continued on through 1955 and many ended the same way the first had, in recriminations and anger. However, they did bring together Frenchmen and top nationalist leaders and this in itself was remarkable. As Mehdi Ben Barka had said when he first asked Father Martin what he could do for them, the Moroccans had had few means of approaching the French in Morocco, and the talks between the two camps helped reduce the anti-Moroccan feeling of the French community and prepared it for the concessions ultimately made by the Paris government. Father Martin himself, when he arranged meetings between the Moslems and the French, took no active part in the discussions. He occasionally turned the talk to other subjects when the two groups would be on the verge of shouting, but other than that he smiled and kept his counsel.

This was not true when he spoke to the French themselves. When, at a luncheon, a group of Meknes businessmen demanded to know why he was supporting the Moslems against the Christians, Father Martin told them they didn't know what they were talking about. The position of the Church on such cases as the Moroccans' demand for independence, he explained, was perfectly clear in principle: peoples and nations did have the right to govern themselves. Thus, he said, it wasn't that Toumliline was going too far, but that most of the French in Morocco had little regard for Christian justice.

This angered many of his French listeners, but did force them to reconsider their own position. After all, he was one of them, and more than that, he was a priest. After a lecture on Toumliline to six hundred student pilots at the Meknes Air Base, he asked the French Air Force colonel in charge if he approved what the monks were trying to do. When he answered by accusing the monks of being anticolonialist, Father Martin deeply disturbed the officer, just as he had disturbed General Miquel, by saying that the man did not know the difference between a political and a nonpolitical position. "In a given historical time, in a given milieu," the Prior said, "colonialism may be good for a colonialized people. But the Church says that the aspirations of a people for independence are legitimate. After this principle is affirmed *then* we go into politics. It's the *application* of the principle that is a political matter. The principle itself is a principle of justice—these people have the *right* to be independent—and it is not a principle of politics. Should they or should they not be independent, this is a judgment that is within the competence of every single Christian."

The Prior told his community about his conversation with the Colonel. He told them that what he had been doing had at least accomplished one thing almost accidentally, that it had won for them the affection of many of the religious leaders of the Moslem community. When he had begun to see the Grand Sheik of Islam in Morocco, the *Fqih* Bel Larbi el Alaoui, both Colonel Clesca and General Miquel had warned him that he was the worst enemy the Church had in Morocco. They told Father Martin of an incident during a lecture of Bel Larbi to students at the Karaouine University in Fez. The sound of a Catholic church bell drifted into the open courtyard where they sat. "There is your true enemy," the *Fqih* warned his students, "do not rest until it has been driven from your country." After the Prior had become quite intimate with the Moslem theologian he asked him if the story were true. The *Fqih* readily admitted it, but added he had not then been able to distinguish between the Church and French authorities. "But now," he said, "seeing what you do at Toumliline has helped me to make that distinction."

Still later, after many conversations in which each came to understand the essential inspirations of the other's religion, Bel Larbi made a startling admission. "I would respect the conversion of a Moslem to Christianity if made in a certain way." He explained the qualification.

"If a man is convinced of the truth, as you and I are, one measure of that conviction is his desire to share it with others. Thus I am sure you are as desirous of converting me to Christianity as I am to convert you to Islam. But such a desire must always respect the personality and liberty of conscience of the others. The conversion must not be by violence or argument but by the splendor of a life lived according to that truth."

Father Martin told his monks of having met another religious leader, Mohammed el Fassi, at Ben Barka's house. This ardent nationalist, later Minister of Education and Rector of the University of Morocco, was from a patrician family of Fez that had been expelled from Spain by Isabella the Catholic in 1492. In a way, Mohammed el Fassi represented that segment of Moroccan Moslems intransigently hostile toward things Western. He had maintained this position in spite of taking his graduate work in Paris and even after rooming with a student, Jean Daniélou, now a world-famous Jesuit theologian! But now he has completely changed his attitude, Father Martin said, because of three things he felt demonstrated the Church's independence of French colonialist policy in Morocco. One was the pastoral letter of Archbishop Lefèvre to his priests in 1952 outlining the obligations of Christians toward Moslems in Morocco. Another was the national examination of conscience taken by many French Catholics led by François Mauriac. The final event was our giving tea to those political prisoners.

"This breaking down of centuries-old prejudices," Father Martin concluded, "is one reason for our presence here. If in performing this work of Christ we scandalize Christians who would like the Church to identify itself with certain political policies, it is unfortunate, tragic even, but absolutely necessary."

CHAPTER 9

DURING the early days of hectic construction when the monks and local workmen toiled side by side to convert the school into something more like a monastery, Father Charles, the infirmarian, treated their cuts and bruises. The news spread and soon he had a clientele coming from Azrou and Berber villages twenty miles away. Most of the patients were women and small children. Their needs were obvious—tuberculosis, malnutrition, glaucoma, poor hygiene—but the monks had neither the supplies nor the medical competence to fill those needs. Father Charles had many years practical experience as a nurse but he was not a doctor. (This versatile monk had drawn up the architectural plans for the church at En-Calcat.) At the time Father Martin was considering the remote possibility of hiring a doctor—the monastery actually had no money to pay for one—a young French doctor, Gerald Martignac, asked to join their community.

At first they received the sick in a passageway near the refectory. Soon the crowds grew unmanageable and the noise of Berber conversations and wailing babies shattered the monastic silence. The monastery's chronicle describes the situation on June 28, 1954:

> The crowds keep growing every day. Now we find the women lined up early in the morning at the foot of the stairs leading to our dormitory cells. They take their places with the tenacity of Londoners waiting for the royal coronation procession to pass. As we go to the refectory for breakfast after our Masses, the narrow passageway is overrun by Father Charles' clients. The little Moroccan boy charged with sweeping up the area is filled with joy at assuming the important role of ordering all the women to clear a path for us. A few feet away at the edge of the forest donkeys and mules wait patiently for their masters and mistresses.

It was not until 1955 that funds were available to build a separate dispensary for the patients who sometimes numbered one hundred a day. Begun in April, the low four-roomed building designed by Brother Jean-Michel in local cedar wood and basalt rock was completed by July. Its location alongside the road and over one hundred yards from the Chapel shut off the unfamiliar sounds of women and children from the monastic cloister.

Along with the dispensary, the monks built a home for their growing family of orphaned and abandoned Moroccan children who began arriving in early 1953. After the first summer, the children returned to the monastery on school holidays for games, lessons, and meals. They would arrive early in the morning, usually in groups of twenty or thirty—one day they numbered 187. Some would play soccer or checkers, others would ask the monks to hear their school lessons. At noon, as many as could fit ate with the monks in the refectory. The overflow would sit under the trees, four to a platter of *tajine* (usually a lamb stew) which they would eat with their fingers. Two Arabic-speaking monks, Father Gilbert and Brother Eugene, were given the job of looking after the boys.

As these monks came to know the children, Father Martin made a decision that committed the monks to a work they had not foreseen in coming to Toumliline. Soon twenty youngsters ranging in age from ten to fifteen years were lodged at the monastery. Father Martin became their legal guardian and assumed responsibility for their upbringing. Four of the brightest were sent to secondary schools, returning "home" to Toumliline for vacations. The younger ones were enrolled in Moslem primary schools in Azrou, hiking back and forth each day over the steep mountain short cut with their lunch and school books strapped to their backs. Older boys with no schooling were sent as apprentices to learn carpentry and gardening. One of these, an eleven-year-old deaf-mute, became Brother Jean-Michel's assistant gardener.

For all these children Toumliline became the center of their "family" life. Father Gilbert was treated by the children with the same respect and docility reserved by all Moroccan children for their fathers, and he ruled them with a firm hand. With Brother Eugene though, the boys would cut up and act as with an older brother.

From the beginning, the monks scrupulously respected the religious faith of these young Moslems. In fact, contact with the monks quickened the boys' own faith and they began, for example, to keep the month-long fast of Ramadan at an earlier age than required by Koranic law. Some Azrou parents, whose children used to visit Toumliline during the day, sent a delegation to Fez to consult the *Fqih,* Bel Larbi, asking him if there was anything wrong or dangerous in allowing their children to visit these Christian monks. "Not at all," the theologian reassured them. "They are men of God."

Contact with young Moroccans showed Father Martin the dilemma they faced. Coming from families with traditions unchanged for centuries, these youngsters suffered terrible confusion in the face of the new. One graduate of the Berber College in Azrou told the Prior he did not want to rejoin his family. His illiterate father was a mountain shepherd, he agonized, and his mother, like every woman of the region, lived out her life carrying wood and water for the family and weaving rugs. The young man, though he refused to go home, confided to Father Martin the fear he would lose his faith which seemed so tied to the ancient ways.

This contact with Moroccan youth was greatly extended in the summer of 1955 when a number of vacation camps were opened in the hills surrounding Toumliline. Students attending these camps came from as far away as Marrakech, Casablanca, and Rabat as well as from nearby Meknes and Fez. They were French and Moroccan, Jewish and Moslem. Many of them would hike to Toumliline, eat their lunch under the trees, and then join the monks for coffee and conversation. The Moslem students delighted at the openness of the monks. For many of them, it was their first friendly personal contact with Frenchmen. The French authorities, however, were not at all pleased at the ardent nationalism displayed by these Moroccans—they were forever singing *Istiqlal* songs, even at Toumliline—and after two weeks ordered the Moslem camps shut down.

This order was symptomatic of the worse-than-ever political crisis of 1955. The Moroccan terrorists stepped up their activities prior to August twentieth, second anniversary of the Sultan's exile. French counterterrorists grew bolder and, at least in Casablanca, operated with the complicity of the local French police. A French hero of World War II, Pierre Clostermann, who advocated "a dialog between Moroccans and French," left the country after repeated bombings of his home. A French lawyer, Jean-Charles Legrand, who had narrowly escaped a French lynch mob after defending some accused Moroccan terrorists, was arrested after he shot three French counterterrorists when they attempted to assassinate him. Even after eighty murders attributed to counterterrorists in Casablanca, not a single arrest had been made. An American correspondent quoted one policeman as saying, "What? Arrest Frenchmen for killing these Moroccan pigs? They ought to be given the Legion of Honor!"

They went too far, however, with the June machine gun killing of Jacques Lemaigre-Dubreuil, a personal friend of French Premier Edgar Faure and an advocate of a moderate policy of "evolutionary autonomy" for Morocco. The Paris government began to investigate the Casablanca police department and discovered that some of its top officials were key members of counterterrorist organizations.

Shocked into action, Premier Faure replaced the well-intentioned but ineffectual Francis Lacoste with Gilbert Grandval as the new Resident General.

Arriving in Morocco early in July, Grandval's first move was to discharge ten French officials of the protectorate administration. Next, on Bastille Day, he declared a general amnesty, released hundreds of political prisoners, and promised to close down all detention camps. The French extremists reacted immediately, turning his personal appearances into near riots. In Casablanca he was spat upon and manhandled as the police looked on. The French crowd shouted epithets like "Grandval to the gallows." In Meknes, the police even shot into a crowd of five hundred young Moroccans come to greet the new Resident General, killing thirty and wounding 250. Shaken, Grandval cancelled the rest of his inaugural tour and fired off a report to Paris warning that unless the French extremists could be curbed and the deposed Sultan returned before August Twentieth there would be a general uprising.

With French night patrols shooting anything that moved in the Moroccan sections of the larger cities, the Moslem students from the closed vacation camps were reluctant to return home. Having sampled the easygoing hospitality of the monks, they descended on Toumliline by the hundreds. The monastery's guest cells and a converted garage were quickly filled and Father Martin had to borrow three large tents from the Beni M'Guild tribe. Chaplains from the American air and naval bases in Morocco arranged for the loan of surplus blankets—the temperature drops forty degrees during the chilly mountain nights. Outdoor kitchens were set up and cooking chores were handled by the scouts among the students. Groups of thirty were rotated regularly so each could eat in turn with the monks in the refectory. But this created special problems because the monks keep silence while they eat, listening to readings from the Holy Rule of St. Benedict, Sacred Scriptures, and books of current interest. Father Martin called all the boys together and explained the reasons for this. After that, they scrupulously observed the rule of silence whenever they entered the cloistered part of the monastery.

The Prior arranged with foreign visitors to Toumliline to meet groups of the Moroccan students at informal after-dinner teas. Foreign journalists, American servicemen and even an official of the *Union Française,* France's postwar name for her colonial empire, took part in these exchanges. One popular guest was the director of a nearby Jewish camp who had newly returned from Israel. Several times his camp took in an overflow of Moslem students from Toumliline.

In an attempt to satisfy the students' desperate thirst for learning of any kind, Father Martin organized lectures. Father Fulcran taught astronomy and took the boys on geological field trips. Father Pius taught a course on the history of music. Other monks lectured on their specialties and tutored some who had failed baccalaureate examinations. So intent were the young Moroccans, they even attended a lecture on some obscure nineteenth-century French poets.

Meanwhile new developments on the political front

threatened Toumliline. The French army had received numerous reports that a Berber "Army of Liberation" was being recruited and trained in the Atlas mountains. The chief organizer was supposed to be Mahjoubi Aherdane, the Berber nationalist and former French army captain whom the Prior had met at the home of Mehdi Ben Barka. In addition, it was rumored that representatives of the newly begun Algerian revolution were attempting to enlist this new army in a joint campaign to sweep the hated French into the sea. As Father Martin put it,

> Things were relatively tranquil for us because we were on excellent terms with our Moroccan neighbors in the Middle Atlas mountains. One thing troubled me, however. A band of these soldiers fired up with anti-French hatred could sweep up from the Moroccan-Algerian Sahara and wipe out all my monks without our Moroccan friends knowing what was happening. And while every monk retires at night prepared not to see the morning, I warned them of its immediate possibility.

These reports of the formation of a Berber army particularly disturbed the local French because their propaganda had pictured Morocco's four million country Berbers as staunchly loyal to France and bitterly opposed to Sultan Mohammed V. Should the Berbers make common cause with the more urban *Istiqlal,* it would mean a full scale war against the French.

In Azrou, Colonel Clesca's men constantly patrolled the hills around Toumliline looking for concentrations of Berber horsemen. Occasionally they would ask Father Martin if he hid such or such a man at the monastery. One day when the monks were in chapel chanting the divine office a jeepload of armed French soldiers drove up to the gate. They piled out, guns at the ready, and headed across the monastery grounds. Father Gilbert, singing by a window, was closest to the chapel door. Stepping out of his choir stall, he bowed toward the altar tabernacle, turned and streaked out the door. Intercepting the men he furiously ordered them away. "No one enters this monastery carrying a gun!" he told them.

Nationalist feeling was running high around Azrou, especially among the Berbers. Propaganda was being fed them in Berber-language broadcasts from Cairo, Spanish Morocco, and Hungary urging them to rise up against the French. Almost every tent and house had a battery powered radio tuned to these stations all day long. When the men returned home at the end of a day, their women inflamed them with the latest broadcasts. As one Berber horseman told his friend, Father Gilbert, "We have suffered enough at the hands of the French. We can take no more. Soon we will kill all Frenchmen."

As the August twentieth anniversary of the Sultan's exile approached, Resident General Grandval shuttled back and forth between Paris and Rabat trying to convince the Cabinet that some drastic, dramatic concessions had to be made. But a general strike, the ritual of August vacations, and a determined "Moroccan Lobby" prolonged the indecision of the government in its negotiations with Moroccan nationalists over the future of the exiled Sultan. For two dramatic days, August Twelfth and Thirteenth, the Resident

General pleaded with the Parliamentary Committee For North Africa, describing the highly volatile psychological state of the Moslem population and the significance they gave to "the fateful date," August twentieth. He demanded a spectacular gesture toward Morocco before that date. The "Moroccan Lobby" representing *colons* and French investors in Morocco got support in their opposition to Grandval's proposals from conservative militarists who saw a terrible loss to France's military prestige in appearing to yield to a nationalist ultimatum. They calmly suggested an August Twenty-fourth meeting with nationalist representatives. Grandval returned to Morocco with his letter of resignation on Premier Faure's desk.

During the day of August Nineteenth there was calm in Azrou. It was a Friday, the Moslem Sabbath, but the mosque was empty. The faithful still refused to pray in the name of the new Sultan. The streets of Azrou were deserted except for patrolling French dragoons. At his command post Colonel Clesca dusted off his plans for the defense of the European community which he had outlined to Father Martin three years earlier. He was saddened, however, by the situation. Although he believed he had sufficient modern military force to deal with the local tribes, he had come to understand something of Father Martin's point of view. A frank and friendly man, he knew all the people in his territory, both little and big. He met them in the streets of Azrou and visited them in the country. He had an awareness of their problems and a true picture of the political situation uncolored by official French propaganda. But while this big ruddy-faced

Colonel agreed that the aspirations of the Moroccans for independence were just, he sincerely thought that the mass of the people were not ready for it. To this extent he felt justified in harassing the local *Istiqlal* members.

Ironically, it was these same *Istiqlal* men who were busy that day touring the mountain areas, arguing with Berber leaders that now was not the time to strike. A premature rebellion, they said, would simply play into French hands. Throughout the entire Middle Atlas, however, the Berbers stood poised to attack. The night of the Nineteenth, the monks spotted fires blazing on the hills overlooking Azrou, the signal for the Berber horsemen to ride. "We went to sleep not knowing if we would live through the night," Dom Denis says.

Thanks in part to the *Istiqlal,* the Beni M'Guild tribesmen did not answer the call that night. Many other neighboring tribes did, though, and on the Twentieth Berber horsemen attacked the village of Oued Zem, about eighty miles southwest of Toumliline. Over ninety European men, women, and children were massacred. Khouribga, in the same area, and Khenifra, forty-eight miles from Toumliline, were also attacked in force. French retaliation was swift and severe. Four days later they had killed over a thousand Moroccans. French Premier Edgar Faure took to the radio and issued a call for 60,000 reservists to serve in Morocco.

When Father Martin learned of the call to the colors he knew it could mean the end of Toumliline if those of his monks among the eligible reserves took up arms against Moroccans. The Prior called the community together and told them why he would oppose the mobilizing of anyone from the monastery. He said he would see the Archbishop immediately.

He drove into Rabat by himself. When he sat down with Msgr. Lefèvre he said, "Your Excellency, I will not allow my monks to answer a call to the colors that would have them fight against Moroccans."

The Archbishop informed the Prior some of his own priests had also been ordered up and that he had been considering what to do about it.

The Prior in turn said, "It is preferable we act together, but as for me, I am irrevocably opposed to the mobilization in principle and I will not allow my monks to serve."

"Take whatever steps are necessary. Do so in both our names."

Father Martin went to the Residency office in Rabat which handled the mobilization and told the Colonel in charge that "I cannot have my monks respond to this call to arms."

The officer was shocked. "But *mon Père,* that is impossible! While there are exceptions granted in certain cases, the law provides none for the clergy."

The priest turned to leave. "Colonel, I must honestly tell you that when I return to the monastery I will order my monks not to answer the call."

"In that event you must see the new Commander in chief, General Miquel."

Father Martin had not yet heard of Miquel's promotion. The former chief of all French forces in Morocco, General Duval had just been killed in an airplane crash while directing the attack against the Berbers at Oued Zem. The

Prior was ushered into the general's immense office and faced his former antagonist across a long bare table that reminded him of a landing strip. This was the first time, he thought, Miquel looked completely at home. After they were seated, he outlined his problem to Miquel.

The general paused before answering the priest. He could overlook the business of giving tea to the nationalist prisoners as the mistake of a naive monk, but he could never forgive the Prior for befriending his enemy, the *Istiqlal* organizer of Meknes, Driss M'Hammedi.

"*Mon Père,* I cannot permit you to do this. I have great need of monks in my army. It is good for the morale of my men to know they have men of God serving beside them." Miquel then began to lecture Father Martin on the important role monks have played in the history of wars. After five minutes of this the Prior was furious.

"I understand your point of view very well, general, but I have my own point of view as well. They are not the same. I have the responsibility for my community. I positively refuse to allow my monks to answer the mobilization." The Prior turned and walked out.

That night Father Martin flew to Paris and next morning was at the War Ministry asking to see Brigadier General Jean Lecomte. The general, however, was at Aix-les-Bains taking part in the government meetings with Moroccan nationalists negotiating the future of Sultan Mohammed V. His adjutant, Colonel Jarrot, received the Prior kindly.

"My monks are being called to the army in Morocco," Father Martin began. "You know why we are there. There is an absolute contradiction. Our mission cannot be compromised in this way. Therefore, I wish to inform the general that my monks will not serve."

The colonel picked up a phone with a direct line to Aix-les-Bains and explained the Benedictine's position to the general. Lecomte came up with a compromise: the monks must submit to the mobilization, but they will remain mobilized *within* the monastery. He then extended the ruling to all the clergy of Morocco. After the general's office had phoned Miquel in Rabat informing him of this arrangement, the exhausted Prior headed for home.

Seventy-two hours later soldiers from Azrou arrived with orders to pick up the monks who had refused to answer the mobilization call. The Prior excused himself for a moment and placed a call to Paris. Coming out of his office, he told the young lieutenant in charge what he had done, and that Rabat would be calling shortly to cancel his orders. At this a sergeant exploded.

"How much more are we going to take from this monk! Let's not argue with him. Let's just hang him!"

The sergeant meant it, for many of the French military at that time looked on Father Martin and the monks as traitors. When General Miquel later left Morocco he spread many uncomplimentary reports about Toumliline, particularly among Benedictines in France. On a business trip to En-Calcat, Toumliline's sub-Prior, Father Jean-Marie, was surprised to hear one of the monks say, "We have heard of the dirty politics you are playing in Morocco." When Jean-Marie protested that this was not so, the monk replied, "You can't tell me anything I don't already know. My brother in the army is stationed in Azrou and his assignment is to keep track of your maneuvers."

Most realistic Frenchmen, however, realized a mistake had been made in deposing the Sultan, and that his hand-picked successor, Mohammed VI, would have to leave the throne before there would be any peace. This was behind the French government's negotiations with Si Bekkai and other representatives of Mohammed V at Aix-les-Bains. The stalemate in those talks was dramatically broken when, in late October, El Glaoui, arch foe of the former Sultan, suddenly reversed himself and demanded his return to the throne. Mohammed V was flown to France from his exile in Madagascar and a great wave of joy swept his country. Delegations from all over Morocco headed for Paris to do homage to their exiled sovereign.

Father Martin was in Paris the week of the Sultan's triumphant visit. A telegram arrived from Driss M'Hammedi asking that he reserve forty-eight hotel rooms for a delegation from the Middle Atlas. The Prior not only found the rooms, he even rented a bus to meet them at Orly airport at three o'clock in the morning. Many of Toumliline's closest friends were in the delegation, including the venerable *Fqih* Bel Larbi el Alaoui. Because of the *Fqih's* prestige—he had been the only one of the *Oulema* to vote against the election of Mohammed VI, thus legally voiding it—the Sultan granted his delegation an immediate audience. The Moroccans insisted that Father Martin come along. He gently refused their invitation and explained why. "Up till now," he told them, "I have been helping some of my good friends in a private matter. To visit the

Sultan *at this time* would mean participating in a public political action. This I cannot do."

By now disorders in Morocco had become so widespread the French asked Mohammed V to return to the throne. His first government read like the guest book at Toumliline: M'Barek Si Bekkai was Prime Minister; Driss M'Hammedi was a Minister of State and then Minister of the Interior; Mehdi Ben Barka was President of the National Consultative Assembly; Mohammed el Fassi was Minister of Education; Captain Mahjoubi Aherdane was Governor of Rabat.

Shortly afterwards, Prince Moulay Hassan paid a royal visit to Azrou, his first since his father's exile. Tents were set up in the center of town and Berbers descended from the hills to see their prince. The red Moroccan flag with its green star was displayed from every balcony and lamppost. The French tricolor was conspicuous by its absence.

A royal summons came to the monastery bidding Father Martin to come to Azrou. The Prior descended in a government car flying the royal flags. As he approached the reception tent, he spied a delegation of the local French population of small business men, teachers, and minor civil servants. Expecting to join them, he was surprised when the Caid of Azrou escorted him past the group on toward the prince. At this point a young French colonel marched out from the crowd, smiling and extending his hand to the Prior.

Father Martin recognized him as the new commandant of French forces billeted in the area. He had come to Azrou several months earlier at about the same time

Colonel Clesca had been transferred to another post. Ignoring local tradition the new commandant had never bothered to call on the Prior and had made clear to others his low estimate of the monk's patriotism. Now, as he stepped forward with outstretched hand, he seemed anxious to appear before the crowd as an intimate friend of the Prior. Father Martin, however, turned inquiringly to the Caid who made a show of introducing the chagrined French officer to his countryman and co-religionist.

Moving on, Father Martin was taken to a place alongside the prince. Moulay Hassan thanked the Prior in the name of the Sultan for the friendship and understanding the monks had shown Moroccans during the troubles. Royal protocol called for the prince to retire to the royal tent alone during the tremendous feast prepared by the Beni M'Guild tribe. However, he invited Father Martin and the government ministers present to share his tent. The frustrated Colonel ate in another tent with the French delegation.

During the feast the prince recalled his earlier visit to Toumliline. He had dropped in unexpectedly one day in August, 1953, and been shown around the monastery. Si Bekkai had told the Sultan about Father Martin and the orphans, and the prince had come to see for himself. He had addressed these young Moroccans saying, "You can trust these fathers. Like true fathers they love you and will teach you nothing but good." These words spoken by a descendant of the Prophet and heir of the spiritual leader of Morocco's nine million Moslems, had brought tears to the eyes of the Benedictine monk. Afterwards, the prince made arrangements for his father to visit Toumliline the following week. This visit never took place because the following week the Sultan, accompanied by Moulay Hassan, was flown off to exile.

Many official feasts followed this one and in each case the same pattern was followed. A government car would call at the monastery for the Prior and he would be given a place of honor at the affair. Some Frenchmen reproached Father Martin for this and said that he was injuring the dignity of France by consorting with the Moroccans now in power. Father Martin's answer was always the same: "I am a guest in a foreign country, and if a government official invites me to dinner, I should go."

Then the *Istiqlal* party held a giant victory feast in Azrou. The chiefs of the party came from Casablanca, Rabat, Fez, and Meknes. The Prior received an invitation from its leader, Allal el Fassi, to attend. Father Martin sent back word to the most powerful political figure in the country that he would not. "Please tell Monsieur Allal el Fassi that I do not involve myself in politics. Tell him also that I will welcome him at the monastery any time he cares to visit."

CHAPTER 10

THE year 1956 brought a threat of great physical danger to the monks of Toumliline. The French military had abdicated official authority in the country, but seemed half-ready to assert their strength if the Sultan failed to achieve civil order. Moroccan irregulars seemed constantly trying to goad the French troops into a fight. French soldiers were being ambushed and killed around Azrou. The entire Middle Atlas area was in a turmoil. Travelling out of the area was a problem. Seven roadblocks manned by armed Berbers were thrown up between Azrou and Meknes. Going into the Middle Atlas mountains was something few dared to do. Rumors were constant in Rabat and Casablanca that the monks had been wiped out.

Yet the tranquility that is the heritage of Benedict never deserted his sons in Morocco. One day Dom Charles told Dom Placide, the ebullient cellarer, that one of his patients that day at the clinic had been a Berber from the Moroccan Army of Liberation. The infirmarian explained that the soldier had been shot in the leg during a skirmish with the French and that he had extracted the bullet. "He was so grateful," Charles said, "that he wanted to know if he could kill one of my enemies for me. Even more than one if I wanted."

"What did you say?" Placide asked.

"I told him, of course, there was no one I wanted killed."

"You told him that!" Placide shouted indignantly. "You should have referred him to me. I would have given him the names of our creditors!"

Dom Placide, a native of Orleans, had taken over the job of cellarer the previous fall from Dom Gilbert, who was now forced to spend most of his time with the orphans. Placide had last been in Morocco the middle of 1953. It was then that he had flown back to his home monastery, En-Calcat, after recovering from a seven-month bout with tuberculosis. However, once back in France, he began to badger his abbot to assign him permanently to Dom Denis' foundation. And finally when Rome raised Toumliline to the status of an independent priory, the Abbot, bringing along the happy thirty-three-year-old Placide, departed for Morocco to formally install Dom Denis as the elected Prior of Toumliline. Still Placide might not have been able to stay had not one of the Toumliline monks, Dom Ambroise, exercising his right, withdrawn from the Moroccan community to return to En-Calcat, the monastery in which he had taken his vows as a Benedictine. With this, Placide petitioned the Prior for admission to Toumliline and was accepted.

It was fortunate for Toumliline that he had been accepted. For Dom Placide, a man who had found in the cloister the immeasurable room his personality needed to expand and express itself, was a born improvisor with a fantastic capacity for work and a willingness to accept any responsibility in any amount. Dom Denis, worn out by work and plagued by the need for money, recognized that the tall, thin monk with the grey eyes and the constant smile was just the one to shoulder all the economic problems of the community.

As was the case with many of the monks of Toumliline, Placide had developed an impressive string of talents during his sixteen years as a Benedictine. He was an electrician, mechanic, farmer, writer, printer, editor, stonemason, builder, linguist, and bookkeeper. And what he may have sometimes lacked in finesse he made up in flair. Everything Placide did he did with speed and dash. Thus when someone suggested that ninety-five miles an hour was not a good speed to travel along a Moroccan road, his smiling answer was: "There are only two kinds of drivers, those that fear and those that cause fear!" This attitude carried over into every one of his activities. For example, when Toumliline would have no money in either of the two banks it did business with, Placide would write out a check for whatever amount was needed, explaining that "the banks and I have an understanding. They always honor my checks, no matter how much I am overdrawn. At the end of every month, I receive statements telling me how much I owe. This saves me the formality of a loan."

Placide's hectic calm wasn't ruffled when the Prior informed him in March, 1956 that the Moroccan government had agreed to co-sponsor an international seminar at Toumliline the coming summer. The purpose of the meeting, Dom Denis said, was to help repair the cultural ties between Morocco and Europe that had been broken by the years of political unrest. The Prior asked Placide to handle all the details of the three-week seminar: invite a hundred or so participants, determine what lectures would be given and how they should be scheduled, and arrange the housing and feeding of visitors. The Prior pointed out that the assignment would include building a lecture hall, a guest house, and a dining hall as well as raising the money for this construction. Placide and Brother Jean-Michel then figured out the buildings would cost seventeen and a half thousand dollars. The young cellarer wondered where he would get the money.

In April a French industrialist promised the monastery the total sum. But later, when the buildings were half completed, Placide found out the industrialist had withdrawn his offer. "As builder, this did not bother me," Placide says. "We had already bought on credit the equipment and material we needed. But as cellarer I was shocked. I had to *pay* for everything."

Something much more crucial than money preoccupied Dom Denis the first half of 1956. It was the survival of Toumliline. True, the Sultan had returned to his throne and the protectorate had been ended. Nonetheless, the chances of a military showdown between France and Morocco persisted. The French, reluctant to completely abandon this "conservatory of the grandeur of France" and anxious to flank an Algeria now suffering the agony of civil war, insisted on maintaining more than 50,000 troops in Morocco. And while Mohammed V, who had no army of his own, could do nothing about this, there did exist in Morocco a non-French force dedicated to the expulsion of France from both Morocco and Algeria. This was the 45,000-man Army of Liberation, constituted mainly of Berbers. This army was concentrated in the Middle Atlas Mountains. Its headquarters in the Azrou area was located on a farm adjoining Toumliline.

Complicating the picture even more was the problem of the 350,000 French civilians in Morocco. Ninety thousand of them made up the backbone of the administrative and technical apparatus in the country. Understandably enough, both the French government and the Sultan wanted these 90,000 to stay where they were, the former because it did not want to see these people flooding back into France, the latter because he desperately needed them to run the country. But would these people stay—this was the problem. Could they adjust to life in a country they no longer controlled? Did they want to adjust? And if they did stay, what guarantee would there be that once a Moroccan cadre was formed they would not be thrown out of their jobs?

The Prior's position was that the French civilians should gamble on the good will and the good sense of the Moroccans. He pointed out that if the French in Morocco did *not* support the Sultan and affirm their faith in the future of his country, it could lead to the collapse of his government, the reimposition of the protectorate and then full-scale war between the French forces in Morocco and the Army of Liberation.

To demonstrate what he meant, the Prior went ahead with plans to organize the annual Pentecost pilgrimage of

French Catholic students to Toumliline. Patterned after the students' pilgrimage to Chartres in France, the Toumliline pilgrimage had attracted hundreds of young Catholics in 1954 and 1955. Now when more than three hundred had signed up, suddenly the affair was off: the parents of the students feared that the Army of Liberation would attack the group.

Dom Denis then had a notice, addressed to "Young Christians," printed in the French-language newspapers of Morocco. It asked that the students

> . . . come to Toumliline to reflect on the meaning of your presence on Moroccan soil and to pray for the future of the new Morocco. Come in great numbers! It is essential for Morocco that understanding, generous young Christians show the way to those who are disturbed, frightened, and discouraged. Come with confidence! You often hear it said the Middle Atlas Mountains are not safe. The monks say to you: "We live here; we invite you to come without fear." Our Moroccan friends know you come here to pray for them. They know this is your gesture of love for their country and their people. God will bless the faith and enthusiasm that you direct toward the welfare of the Moroccan community.

Two hundred and fifty Catholics answered the appeal. On the eve of Pentecost buses left Casablanca and Rabat. At Ifrane early the next morning the 250 young men and women shouldered their knapsacks and started the twelve-mile march through the cedar and oak forests toward the monastery. As they sang the miles away, they saw armed horsemen riding the ridges above them.

The Archbishop of Rabat greeted the students at Toumliline when they arrived at eleven o'clock, thanking them on behalf of the French of Morocco for making the pilgrimage. He led them to a spot in the woods a hundred yards below the monastery where a stone altar had been built and said Mass. By the time it had ended, a dozen armed Berbers had set up a perimeter around them. A girl from Casablanca asked Dom Denis why they were there, and he told her they had been assigned to protect the pilgrims.

That night the 250 pitched tents around the monastery as the soldiers continued to stand guard. After Mass and breakfast, the pilgrims boarded the buses that had come down from Ifrane and headed back toward the coast. Just before she left, the girl who had spoken to the Prior previously thanked him for arranging for the guards. "I don't know why *anyone* stayed away," she said. She pointed at the soldiers: "With those men protecting us, we had no reason to fear the Army of Liberation."

"They *belong* to the Army of Liberation," the Prior said.

The Prior did not explain to her that the pilgrims' entire line of march from Ifrane had been patrolled by the Army of Liberation, nor that its men had guarded key points all the route from Rabat and Casablanca. This detail had been arranged by two friends of Dom Denis—Minister of the Interior Driss M'Hammedi and Mahjoubi Aherdane, Governor of the Province of Rabat and principal creator of the Army of Liberation. It was Aherdane, poet, painter, ex-French Army captain, and most popular Berber in the country, who had actually gone to the Middle Atlas and had asked local commanders to guard the pilgrims.

Another gesture made by the prior to promote friendship between the Moroccans and the French was Toumliline's international summer seminar, a project that had Dom Placide frantic from March. This three-week affair started August Seventh, only hours after the lecture hall, guest house, and dining hall had been finished. That next morning the lecturers and students began to arrive. By midmorning the 120 registered members of the seminar were at the monastery, as well as 850 opening day guests, newspaper writers and photographers from European and Moroccan papers, and official Moroccan, French, British, Austrian, Swedish, Canadian, and American representatives. Ceremonies began with a huge *diffa* given by members of the Beni M'Guild Tribe. They set up their turtle-backed black tents, roasted sheep in mud and dung ovens, and sang the Berber songs their forebears had sung in Spain centuries before.

In the afternoon, Dom Denis, standing in front of a microphone on the concrete speakers platform, addressed the crowd that packed the lecture hall, spilled out into the passageway, and into the covered entrance and garden that sided the hall. As water sprinkled into the blue-tiled fountain that separated the lecture hall from two adjoining conference rooms, the Prior bade everyone welcome. And then running true to form, he immediately defined his position and the position of the monastery concerning the seminar.

> When the Benedictine monks [he started], at the request of Monsignor Lefèvre, set out for Morocco they did not know the demands that would be made on them. They knew they would continue the life they had been following. For the monk, wherever he goes, always seeks the same goal: to glorify God as much as he can. St. Benedict in his Rule describes this ideal as a *return to God.* This involves the total gift of oneself realized progressively by submission to divine grace. The monk is the man who offers himself totally to the transforming action of God through His Church, and forces himself by means of the cloister to eliminate from his life any conflicting influence.

He went on to add that monasteries were the Church in miniature and that they, like the Church, adapted themselves in the countries in which they existed.

> In coming to Morocco [he observed] we did not know how the country would mold us, since it was so new to us, since we knew practically nothing about it. We knew the Church already had its place here. Islam is tolerant; one could easily show that by the history of Morocco. We knew we would be well received and we were not wrong: the people of this country, as well as its great lords have devotion and respect for what is sacred.

The Prior then mentioned the talk that Pope Pius XII and the Crown Prince Moulay Hassan had had in early 1956 in Rome. This talk, the Prior said, resulted in the joint conclusion that "in the face of the harmful percepts of materialism, which are a threat to civilization, we wish to establish bridges between the Moslem and Christian worlds.

Then the Prior explained:

> This is exactly what the Benedictines of Toumliline are trying to do in their own way. In other times people ignored each other, they lived apart, they suffered from the illusion they were self-sufficient and without need of others. And as one dislikes what one does not know, they hated each other. But today the wonderful ease of communication opens horizons; people are forced to see they depend on one another. They are forced to recognize what they have in common, of what is universal in each of them, and what ought to permit them to love each other. Similarly, each sees in greater detail and with greater clarity the gifts that are proper to each, those gifts received from God and developed by their ancestors. In these exchanges, they discover in others what might be called their mission and their vocation.

After this, the Prior said:

> The Church wishes only to serve: to serve the faithful, whom she leads to salvation, insofar as they attend to her; to serve also the country in which she is situated. In what way? That's the question I've often asked of our Moroccan friends. Give us contacts, they answered. That is, in fact, one of the great services the Church can offer you. She is from all continents. Seven hundred million Christians—four hundred million Catholics—are scattered over the world; she offers you the friendship, the peculiar and diverse riches of all the children of our common Father, the Most High God, Who is in the Heavens.

From this point, the Prior went on to explain the circumstances that led to the seminar:

> Last summer the monastery was full of Moroccan students from Fez and Casablanca, from the Karaouyine, as well as from lycées and Moslem colleges. We were obliged to improvise courses on subjects that interested them. This year we did not wish to let ourselves be surprised again. This gave us the idea of organizing a summer seminar, then the idea of enriching it by having foreign students take part in it. His Majesty the King did us the great favor of wishing to preside over the honorary committee.

Among the official members of the seminar, the country with the biggest bloc of representatives was Morocco with fifty-three Moslem Arabs and Berbers. France ran a close second with fifty. Then came Germany with eight, Algeria with three, the French Cameroons with three, Madagascar and Belgium and Holland with one apiece. The 120 had gathered at the monastery to discuss the elusive subject, The State. The students among them followed academic disciplines from law to physics to agronomy, from mathematics to medicine to philosophy and theology. There were twenty-three nonstudents, including Mahjoubi Aherdane, Driss M'Hammedi, Mohammed el Fassi (Minister of Education), Mohammed Ben Larbi el Alaoui (Morocco's leading Moslem theologian), Ahmed Balafrej (Minister of Foreign Affairs), Archbishop Amédée Lefèvre, Father Jean Daniélou, Louis Massignon, Louis Gardet, the last two being among the top European Orientalists. There was also Madame Fatima Hassar, the head of the woman's branch of the *Istiqlal,* who spoke to the sessionaires about the need to emancipate Moroccan women from the social law that allowed her to leave her home only twice in her life, the day of her marriage and the day of her burial.

The sessions themselves were divided into formal lectures in the morning, an afternoon of seminars, followed by entertainments in the evenings that included everything from Arabic plays put on by the National Moroccan Theatre to spirituals sung by the Cameroon students. The last evening's entertainment "crowned the whole session," the feminist Fatima Hassar said.

> It had been organized by the Moroccans and consisted of Berber dances and songs. Governor Aherdane read his poems, and Minister Driss M'Hammedi played the tambourine. Governor Aherdane also danced, and all the Moroccan students, as well as everyone else, joined in. In fact, one of the Benedictine fathers (Dom Placide) also danced with complete abandon. All who was there that evening brought away an unforgettable memory of what they experienced.

In its essence, the seminar established the point that both the East and the West were traditionally concerned with what the state could do for the individual rather than what the individual could do for the state. Thus the Sultan when he spoke to the members of the seminar on closing day said:

> . . . this is the first international reunion of its sort held in an independent and unified Morocco. Our country is (for another reason) very happy and proud that the object of your preoccupations had nothing in common with the materialism so evident today. On the contrary, you have searched for the roads which

> lead to the spiritual values which truly permit humanity to advance toward a better world.
> . . . you know that morality, virtue and love of country constitute the foundation of the state in Islam.

The seminar had been interrupted occasionally by Dom Placide to introduce the *sessionaires* to the Morocco outside the Azrou area. Once he drove them by bus to Fez. Another time they traveled to Ksar es Souk over a route that took them 220 miles due south of Toumliline, across the Middle and High Atlas Mountains, to the edge of the Sahara.

The Governor of this region, the Berber Adi ou Bihi, was fighting with the *Istiqlal* because he thought it was trying to usurp the power of the Sultan. He also resented that the *Istiqlal* was sending in men as school teachers and administrators. On the *sessionaires'* way to Ksar es Souk, the *Istiqlal* found out where they were going and arranged it so they would be met by their men. The seminar was famous in Morocco and they thought it would give them prestige in their fight against Adi ou Bihi if they entertained the *sessionaires.* So when they arrived, the *Istiqlal* asked if they would have tea with them at three. Placide accepted. Then Adi ou Bihi sent a messenger and asked them to be at *his* palace at three for tea. The monk decided they would go to both.

When they were at the *Istiqlal* tea, attempts were made to detain the guests because of the invitation from Adi ou Bihi. But all drank their tea quickly and left for the palace of the Governor. On the way, the young Moroccans in the group sang the *Istiqlal* hymn and then refused to accept hospitality. Placide and the others went into the palace alone. After the tea was finished Adi ou Bihi asked them to stop in at another of his palaces on our way back to Azrou but Placide refused.

On their way back to Azrou the caravan did make the mistake of stopping at the palace of the Caid of Midelt. The Caid belonged to the *Istiqlal.* While they were having tea with him a huge crowd of Adi ou Bihi supporters surrounded the palace, shooting off guns, and shouting insults at the Caid. Forgetting the niceties of Moroccan hospitality, Placide led the rush to the buses, and with everyone aboard, they headed north again.

The buses had just reached the outskirts of Midelt when they ran into a roadblock. Telling everyone to stay inside, and especially making it a point to ask the young Moroccans who had sung the *Istiqlal* hymn outside the palace of Adi ou Bihi to stay quiet, Placide hopped out of the lead bus. He was quickly surrounded by armed Berbers. Where was he going, they asked. When he told them, they asked where he was coming from. He said Ksar es Souk. "Do you support the *Istiqlal* or Adi ou Bihi?" they demanded to know.

The monk was worried, for some of the men at the roadblock were so excited they were bouncing up and down like dervishes. Placide held up his hand and smiled and said, "I assure you, my friends, that I am an *absolute* neutral." With this, he climbed back into his bus and ordered the driver to proceed. The Berbers stepped aside as the buses drove toward them.

When the seminar ended, the Moroccan government

asked the Prior to schedule another one for the following summer. There was only one obstacle; he had no money. It was more than possible, he knew, that he could persuade the French and Moroccan governments to entirely support the 1957 *Cours*, but he preferred to have the monastery pay the bulk of the expenses. This would help attract those non-Moroccan specialists unwilling to lend their names and talents to a government-sponsored affair. It would also keep control of the session in the hands of the Prior.

At this point the Prior decided to visit America. Supplied with a round-trip ticket to New York by a friend in Casablanca and armed with the names of internationally famous, and wealthy, American Catholics, he began to study English again. His tutor was a visitor to the monastery, a Belgian Benedictine named Father Felix Biolley, who had served for years in his country's foreign service. He set his departure date for October twenty-fifth.

The timing was bad. Two days before all telephone wires running out of Meknes, which was along his route to the coast, had been cut, and there had been riots in the city. More than fifty French men and women were slaughtered in the streets of Meknes.

The direct cause of this uprising was the capture of the Algerian FLN leader, Mohammed ben Bella, by the French. He had come to Morocco a short time previously to discuss the Sultan's plan for ending the revolt in Algeria. On his way back to his headquarters in Tunisia, the French crew of his plane landed in Algeria, where a team of

French security agents were waiting to arrest him. When this news reached Morocco, the killings started.

This alarming report came from Dom Edouard, the Prior's secretary, who had gone to Meknes on the Twenty-fourth on business. Edouard had quickly left the city when he noticed that no one was on the streets, surmising correctly that the wrath of the Moroccans had been turned against the French because of the ben Bella affair. On his return to Toumliline, he warned the Prior that he had better postpone his trip for a while.

The Prior would not hear of it. On the morning of the Twenty-fifth he said good-by for a second time and got into the monastery Volkswagen. A couple of minutes later he was seen by the monks closely examining the engine. He signalled Father Placide to him.

"What's wrong with the car? It won't start."

Placide looked. "No spark plugs, Father," he said.

"Find Father Edouard!"

A few minutes later Placide was back with the spark plugs and the Prior's secretary. Not a word was said as Placide put the spark plugs back in place. Finally Edouard asked if he could at least see the Prior got safely to Casablanca by driving there with him. The Prior said no. Then Placide asked if he could make the trip to the coast with Dom Denis. Again the Prior refused. "Nothing's going to happen," he promised.

The road to the coast ran straight through Azrou. It was level until the Prior reached a point about five miles from the monastery, then it began to twist and climb toward the top of a plateau, to a point called Ito. Glancing back the way he had come, he made out the red tile roof of Toumliline. Then the full sweep of the plateau came into view. The distant hills that bordered one edge of the plateau were white with thousands and thousands of pitted grey-blue volcanic rocks, making it seem as if they were covered with flowers. Some outcroppings that bordered the road looked like gigantic abstract sculptures. The Prior saw one man working a tiny patch of cleared ground with a wooden plow. And then he saw another one walking across the plateau toward the horizon. A turn in the road and the Prior came across a flock of sheep stained orange from the earth. Another turn and he saw a man beating a donkey that had fallen to the road. Finally he arrived at the town of El-Hajeb. He saw no one, the only living thing being a black and white goat that stood on his hind legs eating leaves from a hedge.

The road took the priest through the wall that had once ringed the town and brought him to the edge of the Plain of Meknes. Off in the distance he saw smoke from a fire. On the outskirts of Meknes he discovered that the smoke came from a burning farm house sitting on a ridge two or three miles away. Then he passed another burning farm, this one only a half mile off the road. A second later he noticed that the house on the adjoining farm was also on fire. At that moment he saw two figures standing on his side of the road, just across from the dirt path that lead to this second burning building. One of them raised his arm in a signal for the car to stop. As the Prior put on his brakes, he noticed that they were two young Berber men.

"We are going to Khemisset," one of the Berbers said in French, naming a town thirty-five kilometres from Meknes. "May we ride with you?"

"Of course," the Prior said. "But what about those farms?"

"They cannot be saved," the same man said. "We were just there and we know."

"But are there not people there?"

"Nobody," the man said, and then in quick, guttural Berber, repeated the conversation to his companion, who apparently knew no French. The second Berber laughed.

Denis opened the door for the two. The non-French-speaking one got in the back seat, the other alongside Martin in the front. Both thanked him for his kindness, the one behind reaching over and shaking his hand awkwardly, then touching his own lips with his hand in the Moroccan manner. The Prior introduced himself as a monk from Toumliline. He asked if they knew the place and they said no. In turn they identified themselves as farm workers on their way back home.

"Is there no work today?" Martin asked.

"No work today, *mon père*," the man next to him said. The man in back tapped his companion's shoulder and asked in Berber what they were talking about, then laughed again when he heard the Prior's question and the answer to it.

"Why is there no work today?" Martin asked.

"Because our *patron* is not home. He and his family were not there when we arrived this morning."

"Which farm were you working on?"

"The one where you stopped for us."

"But that was one of the farms that was burning!"

"Oh yes," he said. Then he smiled pleasantly as he added, "We started the fire ourselves."

The French-speaking Berber translated for his friend in the back seat, who again laughed joyously.

"And did you burn the second farm, too?" the Prior said.

"When we could not find our *patron,* we went to the next farm to ask about him. The people there said he had gone away."

The man in the back punched his companion's shoulder and asked what was going on. He laughed louder than before when he learned the answer.

"Then there were people in the second farm," the Prior said. "What happened to them?"

"We killed them, *mon père.*"

"How many?"

"Just two women."

"Why did you kill them?"

"Because they were French."

At Khemisset the men got out of the Volkswagen and thanked the Prior courteously for the ride. As they disappeared into a store, the Prior drove on toward Rabat.

CHAPTER 11

"YOUR story is touching, Father Martin, but let me show you something."

The Catholic board chairman of a tremendously successful American corporation leaned forward and pressed a button on his desk. "Please bring in the religious file," he asked. A moment later his secretary appeared with a drawer full of cards.

"Do you see these, Father? Each card has the name of a priest or nun who has approached me for money. What do you think of *that*?" he said triumphantly.

"I think you must be very rich."

Father Martin had not realized when he arrived in the United States that he was just one of 2,000 bishops, priests, and nuns who travel hopefully to America every year looking for money for their work. Like them he had sought out the same handful of prominent Catholics. Like most of them, he failed to get what he wanted.

"Don't expect money from those people," advised Bishop Fulton J. Sheen when Father Martin expressed astonishment at the apparent tightfistedness of wealthy Catholics.

"There aren't too many here to begin with, and most of them are already committed to charities." He explained that the bulk of the money he himself collected for the foreign missions came in gifts of one or two dollars.

Although the Prior made absolutely no progress this first month in the United States, it was different in French Canada. Stories on Toumliline were featured in many Canadian papers and Father Martin was interviewed on radio and television. He also lectured at several universities and spoke before religious, fraternal, and businessmen's organizations. Students formed committees to raise money for a delegation of Canadians to attend the next International Summer School. Two medical students made plans to spend their summer vacations as volunteers in Morocco's understaffed hospitals. From his Canadian trip the Prior was able to send five thousand dollars to his anxious cellarer.

But the disappointments continued in the United States. The well-to-do American Catholics he met were invariably enthralled by the story of Toumliline. They would ask him to dinner either in their town houses or at expensive restaurants. Occasionally, they would take him to the theatre. They would then call or write him the following day and say how much they enjoyed his company, how worthy was the work of Toumliline, how unhappy they were for at the moment they could contribute nothing to his monastery. "I would have been delighted to have received just the price of the meal or the theatre tickets," Father Martin says. "I felt like a man who was drowning and suddenly a boat appeared. Then someone leaned out and pushed my head under the water."

Long after his good sense told him that he ought to accept defeat and go home, he stayed on in America. One reason was that he learned from Father Placide that the money from Canada had been spent to pay debts and that the monastery needed more cash quickly. Another reason was that he constantly ran into kindhearted people who would say to him, "Ah, but you must see Mr. X. He is very rich and very Catholic." It would be arranged that Father Martin would meet Mr. X. at a tea or a dinner. Mr. X. would turn out to be indeed rich and Catholic and terribly reluctant to give the Benedictine a penny.

And through it all, too, the priest kept running into the type who would help him . . . for a price. There was, for example, the Canadian businessman who sought him out and offered him $20,000 if he would sign a receipt for tax purposes saying that he had received a gift many times larger from the man. The Prior said he would think it over. The next morning he phoned the Canadian at breakfast and refused. The monk was conscience-stricken that he did not turn down the scheme immediately. By rejecting the offer, he was turning down the one sure chance he had to keep the summer school going. And he was not the only one to think that it was worth perpetuating. The State Department's John Bovey, Jr., Officer-in-Charge of Northwest African Affairs, wrote him, saying, "You are helping to create a means whereby Moroccans may acquire the knowledge for which they hunger and on which their survival and their friendship with the community of free men depend."

There were, though, more pleasant episodes in his New World adventures. Once, for instance, he was standing on a street corner in New York waiting for a bus. He was nervous and ill at ease because he was late for an appointment. Suddenly a red fire chief's car pulled into the curb. The chief jumped out and said, "Hop in, Father." Martin did as he was told. He supposed that there had been a disaster nearby and that a priest was needed. The chief turned and smiled, raising his voice over the noise of the siren and bell, "Where can I drop you off?" The astonished priest gave him the address. Before long he was at his destination.

Another incident that gave his spirits a lift came when he visited the Trappist monastery in Gesthemani, Kentucky. Father Martin had read *The Seven Storey Mountain* by Thomas Merton and wanted to meet this most prolific of American contemplatives. But even though he had a letter of introduction, it was the penitential season of Lent and the ordinarily strict regulations regarding visitors was even stricter. However, as head of another contemplative monastery, Father Martin was extended certain privileges. On a tour of the cloister with the brother in charge of guests, they came to a door behind which came the sounds of a typewriter. The brother said in hushed tones, "Father Merton is writing another book. Would you like to see him?" He gave three soft taps on the door. Immediately there were three loud answering thumps. Timidly opening the door, the brother asked Father Merton in sign language if he would like to meet Father Martin, Prior of a Benedictine monastery in Morocco. Yes, Merton replied in signs, but only if he understands our sign language. Father Martin soon discovered that the Trappist and the Benedictine signs were similar and they "conversed" for an hour. Father Merton told Martin he had heard many good things about Toumliline and wrote on the backs of stray envelopes the names of friends who might help the Prior.

Shortly after this the Prior received a letter from the sub-Prior, Father Jean-Marie, saying that some of the monks were demanding that he come home, that no outside work should keep him away so long from his monastery, that his lack of success in America was a sign that he should abandon the International Summer School.

The day the letter arrived the Prior had an appointment with the Jesuit anthropologist, Father J. Franklin Ewing, Director of Fordham's Institute of Mission Studies and also Director of its Research Services. Despondent, distracted and lonely, he took the subway to the Bronx campus of Fordham—twice getting on the wrong train. As he entered Father Ewing's outer office, somehow the efficiency of the staff added to his sense of inadequacy. Finally ushered into the inner office, he saw the massive Jesuit enthroned behind a huge walnut desk. Wearing a deadpan expression, the American priest appeared formidable. The Prior wondered why he had come to see him. Soon he discovered the deadpan was a running joke Father Ewing played on the world, and he began to feel at ease. They discussed missionary theology and found themselves in complete agreement. So relaxed did Father Martin become that he confided his dilemma to Father Ewing: his community needed him back in the monastery, but if he returned without funds they would have to abandon their International *Cours,* their orphanage, and possibly their dispensary. Thinking aloud in the sympathetic presence of Father Ewing, the Prior decided that Toumliline could not abandon any of these things.

"Do you think I am right?" he asked the Jesuit.

"You couldn't be more right if you were the Archangel Gabriel."

Further encouragement came from Monsignor Edward E. Swanstrom, Executive Director of the American Bishops' Catholic Relief Services. The Prior had only three dollars in his pocket and owed a twenty-six-dollar hotel bill when he arrived in the Monsignor's office. Although the relief agency normally handled only shipments of used clothing and United States surplus food, Msgr. Swanstrom promised Father Martin two thousand dollars in addition to surplus food. And then without saying a word, he opened his desk, took out a checkbook and started writing.

"Here's three hundred bucks, Father. You can't travel around the United States on cigar coupons."

At this point Father Martin decided to return to Morocco. The gift from Monsignor Swanstrom deadened the feeling of defeat. But it was a defeat and he knew it. He had not raised the money for the Summer School. Two of his New York friends, however, persuaded him to stay a few more weeks. They were writing an article on Toumliline for *America,* the Jesuit weekly, and had arranged for an interview by the New York *Times.* They were also busy lining up other magazine, radio, and television publicity for Toumliline.

Almost simultaneously a Canadian friend, Major General George Vanier, wrote to David Rockefeller. The General, former Ambassador to France and Canada's present Governor-General, told him of Father Martin and asked that he see the Moroccan monk. The thorough Mr. Rockefeller checked with the State Department and received a two page appraisal and endorsement of the International *Cours.* The banker then scheduled a half-hour meeting with the Prior.

Father Martin's hopes zoomed. He realized he had been given a second chance. Arriving at the headquarters of the Chase Manhattan Bank, the Prior was ushered into the private offices of David Rockefeller. The banker, tall and smiling, greeted the monk in French and introduced him to his assistant, Richard Dana. The monk spoke of the banker's kindness in seeing him and then began his story of Toumliline. He told the banker why they had come to Morocco, what happened to them during the Moroccans' struggle for independence, the birth of the dispensary, orphanage, and summer school. The half-hour interview stretched into an hour and a half. After the priest had left, Rockefeller turned to Dana and asked, "What do *you* think?"

"He is one of the most impressive men I have ever met."

"Agreed."

A few days later the elated Prior met with three representatives of the Rockefeller Brothers Fund. The gathering, he was sure, was just a prelude to a grant to Toumliline for the summer school. As the conversation gathered momentum, the priest suddenly thought that all the questions were aimed at proving that Toumliline was *not* eligible for a grant from the Fund. The frustration of months suddenly prompted him to remark, "I think that if I were not French and if I were not a priest, I would have no difficulty getting money from you." The meeting ended with the three Fund representatives saying to the dejected monk that they would be in touch with him soon.

They were. Within the week he heard that David Rockefeller would make a personal gift supporting the International *Cours*. The priest later found out that the Fund representatives had recommended this course of action after first confirming their suspicions that Toumliline could not possibly fit any of their current grant programs.

Along with this news the publicity began to break at the beginning of April. The article in *America* and the interview by reporter Wayne Phillips in the New York *Times* were quickly followed by stories in *Newsweek* and *Time* and an article by the Prior himself in *Jubilee*. Many small gifts followed this publicity. Typical was the $35 a non-Catholic secretary collected among her fellow workers after reading the New York *Times* story. A private family foundation put up money to send any four Americans invited to Toumliline. An American bishop made the arrangements enabling a Princeton specialist on Islam, James Kritzeck, to accept Father Martin's invitation to deliver a lecture that summer. A haggard, exhausted, and richer Prior returned to his monks in time for Holy Week.

The week before the opening of the 1957 International *Cours* was every bit as hectic as the first year's opening rush. Brother Jean-Michel fretted at the slapdash way Father Placide's builders were interpreting his meticulous plans. The new construction included a Secretariat building and twelve concrete block chalets, each capable of sleeping ten students. Truckloads of borrowed chairs and tables, mattresses, and blankets had to be unloaded and stored until the buildings were completed. A newly acquired generator, salvaged from a United States airbase junk heap, was coaxed back to operating efficiency by Brother Marie-Antoine who also strung the wiring necessary to connect the chalets with the power plant of the monastery. Brother Jean-Michel sulked for days because no one noticed that a workman had installed one of the colored abstract wall panels upside down in his modernistic Secretariat building.

Father Martin dispensed Father Placide from regular attendance at the monastic hours because of his crushing work load as Secretary of the *Cours*. He was responsible for meeting and transporting to the monastery the more than two hundred participants from twenty-six countries who were arriving different days at both Rabat and Casablanca. He also had to manage the diplomatic protocol involved in greeting Morocco's Crown Prince Moulay Hassan and the Ministers of Foreign Affairs, of the Interior, and of Education. The Ambassadors of the United States, Great Britain, France, and Holland were also expected.

Before dawn on opening day, thousands of Berber men,

women, and children began to converge on Toumliline. They came by donkey, by horse, and by foot. To while away the hours, they sang and danced. About twenty young tribeswomen would line up opposite an equal number of young men and challenge them to a contest of song. The women, many with babies strapped papooselike to their backs, were cloaked in flowing, gaily colored dresses cinched at the waist, and wore silken scarves like turbans. At a signal from a toothless granny squatting before them, the young women, their faces and ankles tattooed with tribal designs, would sing of ancient Berber heroes, of their exploits in love and war. With the fingertips of one hand held before them lightly touching the fingertips of the other, the entire line would slowly undulate to the insistent rhythm of the drums in a refined version of the belly dance.

The young men were dressed in flowing white *djellaba* of ankle-length homespun, their shaved heads wrapped in white turbans, their bare feet shod in heelless, lemon-colored *babouches*. Alternating verses with the women, some groups sang hour after hour without letup.

The crowds lined the road for two miles from the monastery gate behind rows of Berber cavalry in tribal dress seated in polished green and gold leather saddles. When Prince Moulay Hassan arrived at the monastery gate and accepted from Father Martin the traditional sprinkling of rose water and the offering of dates and milk, the crowd roared its approval. "Long live Moulay Hassan!" "Long live his glorious father, Mohammed!" The Berber cavalrymen fired their ancient muskets into the air and the women let loose their spine-tingling, warbling "you-you" cry that defies accurate description. One tiny Japanese girl, standing in the midst of the tumult, could only say: "I am so afraid."

In his inaugural address, Moulay Hassan explained why he had asked Toumliline to devote the '57 *Cours* to the theme, Education.

> It seemed to me [he said] that this topic was the logical corollary of last year's *Cours* on the State. For no man can truly fulfill his obligations to society nor fully enjoy his rights without education. I refer especially to education in a political sense, for this is the most urgent need in Morocco today. We must form good citizens who will have an awareness of the complex social, economic, and political milieu in which they live. And with Morocco preparing for her first general elections, I could not imagine a more timely or more important topic for this *Cours* than Education.

After outlining some of the more urgent educational needs of his country, the Prince welcomed the participants in the name of his father, Mohammed V. "Feel at home in Morocco," he told them, "for in truth every man of good will, every believer is at home wherever he is, because for Christian, Moslem, or Jew, the whole world is, in a sense, the House of God."

Afterwards, students, professors, assorted cabinet ministers and ambassadors, generals, lesser diplomatic officials, the Archbishop of Rabat and the Prince were the guests of the local Beni M'Guild tribe at a *diffa* under the monastery's towering cedars. All morning long, members of the tribe had been slaughtering, dressing, and roasting sheep. The guests were seated in groups of eight around low circular tables under huge tents. Everyone sprawled out, Moroccan style, on luxuriously thick multicolored Berber rugs.

The *diffa* displayed the Moroccan's strong sense of hospitality. The Moroccan students attending the *Cours* carefully divided themselves among the tables to instruct the foreigners in the intricacies of the traditional feast. First came the ritual washing of hands, especially important since eating was from communal dishes using only the first two fingers and thumb of the right hand. Tribesmen circulated among the groups sprinkling everyone with rose water. They were followed by others carrying deep basins and long-necked kettles of hammered copper. Hands were held over the basin, soaped, and rinsed, then dried on towels tucked in the red sashes of the white-robed water bearers. Round loaves of unleavened bread were passed around. For an appetizer, there were platters of skewered sizzling chunks of broiled lamb. The students watched their Moroccan guides tear off a tiny piece of bread to wrap around the hot meat as they slipped it off the end of the skewer. The next course was a whole roast sheep, one for each table.

At one table the host was a bright eighteen-year-old, Mohammed Lamtiri-Larif. He cautioned the others to watch him closely to avoid burnt fingers. Swiftly, he peeled away the crackling hot skin. Then Lamtiri showed how to peel strips of meat with the fingers, and how to get the choice morsels down under the ribs. After explaining that it was the height of rudeness to refuse any food offered by a Moroccan host, he solemnly passed a huge joint to the tiny Japanese girl who "was so afraid." She solved the dilemma by offering it, in turn, to a German boy on her right.

She wondered at the absence of napkins. Once again the cue came from Lamtiri. Between mouthfuls of meat, he would pick off a piece of bread, transferring any excess fat from his fingers to the bread he then ate. He demonstrated another use for the bread during the next course of sliced tomatoes, cucumbers, and six different kinds of olives. With a small piece of bread held with the two fingers, he would pick up a mouthful from the nearest side of the communal dish. In this way, only his thumb touched the food, and only the food that actually went into his own mouth. The most fastidious diner would be satisfied with the almost antiseptic results of this method.

Courses of ripe figs and four varieties of grapes preceded the staple filler of any Moroccan dinner, *cous-cous.* This is a mounded platter of semolina moistened with a hot sauce, sometimes containing skinned grapes and prime bits of roasted sheep. Sheep eyes were reported to be a great Moroccan delicacy so most foreign guests carefully inspected each grape before eating it. As a concession to the non-Moroccans, spoons were provided for this course. They watched, fascinated, as Lamtiri would lift some of the grain between his fingers, drop it into his palm, and with a juggling motion gradually give it a roundish shape. Slightly smaller than a golf ball, it was then tossed into his mouth.

When the tribesmen brought platters of cut up cantaloupe and watermelons, everyone was sure the end had come. It had, but only because Father Martin understood the capacities of his foreign guests and had asked that four of the courses traditionally served at a *diffa* be skipped. The washing basins and kettles came next and the feast ended with several glasses of hot mint tea.

After this exotic introduction to oriental pomp and color, one American professor, Daniel J. Sullivan of Fordham, was amused later that afternoon to see the Beni M'Guild tribesmen take down their nomadic tents and silently steal away—in "job-rated" Dodge trucks.

Even after the Prince, Archbishop, ambassadors and ministers and the huge crowd had left the monastery grounds, there was still plenty of color contributed by the 200 "*sessionaires*" themselves. One of them, Professor James Kritzeck of Princeton, described it this way:

> There was a Japanese who teaches philosophy in Germany, a Dutchman who teaches Spanish in Marrakech, and a Spaniard who teaches music in Holland. There were poets, actresses, sociologists, theologians, photographers, seminarians, pharmacists, psychopathologists, and engineers. There were Belgians with Italian names, Arabs with English names, Germans with French names. There was a yellow-turbaned Moslem theologian from Fez who was actually a Frenchman, a folk singer in blue jeans who was a priest, nuns who were Protestants, and a Persian from Harvard. There was an Imam from a great mosque in Fez, the rector of the French College in Rome, and the son of the president of the World Zionist organiza-

tion. There were great Arabists and little Arabs. The representation from the United States ranged from Princeton, Yale, Marquette, and Fordham to Batten, Barton, Durstine and Osborn.

The next three weeks were filled with lectures, workshops, and informal discussions on various educational topics from the Christian, Moslem, and Jewish points of view. The Christian position was outlined by Father Louis-Marie Regis, O.P. and Professor Olivier Lacombe, deans respectively of the Universities of Montreal and Lille. The Jewish conception of man and his educational goals was presented by Professor Emmanuel Levinas, Director of the Oriental Jewish Teacher's College in Paris. A young, ascetic-looking theologian, Othman Yahya, from the ancient Moslem University of Al-Azhar in Cairo, gave the Islamic view. And while they all touched on their common spiritual heritage from Abraham, each indicated in detail exactly where and how their respective viewpoints differed.

Professors F. S. C. Northrop of Yale and James Kritzeck of Princeton spoke on the interpenetration of Eastern and Western cultures. A French professor, Louis Massignon, who was a friend of the late Charles de Foucauld and is recognized as "Dean of the world's Islamicists," was literally surrounded by students from Arab countries for several hours after his lecture. A Japanese existentialist spoke on Occidental and Oriental humanism and a Swiss Dominican evaluated Marxist theories of education.

One unscheduled discussion highlighted the second week of the *Cours*. It took place at one of Father Martin's daily after-dinner coffee hours, at which small rotated student groups had the opportunity to audit discussions of ambassadors, cabinet ministers and world-famous scholars. That morning's lecture had been given by Mehdi Ben Barka, President of Morocco's National Assembly. He had spoken of the newly founded University of Morocco and of the many problems involved in joining modern educational techniques to traditional Islamic instruction. He had spoken also of Morocco's crash program to reduce its eighty per cent illiteracy rate. Now, over coffee, he said he had received an invitation to visit Red China and inspect the Communists' experiments in basic education. He was anxious to go, he said, because of their apparently spectacular results in wiping out illiteracy among the Chinese peasants. If Morocco was ever to have a stable political life, it would have to educate its masses. "And," the nationalist leader added, "I am ready to use any methods that will produce results." At this point an Indian psychologist, Miss Ika Paul-Pont, related the disappointments of an Indian team of educators who had visited China to learn the Communist methods. For nearly an hour the thirty other guests of Father Martin sipped their coffee and sat fascinated as the beautiful sari-clad Indian and one of Morocco's most powerful political figures argued the respective merits of a democratic and a totalitarian system of education.

During the third week, the visit of the King's eldest daughter, twenty-seven-year-old Princess Lalla Aicha, touched off another colorful demonstration by the surrounding tribes. As on the opening day, huge crowds of singing and dancing people gathered at Toumliline to honor their royal family. The Princess lectured on "The Emancipation of Moroccan Women." Since 1947 her father had made her a symbol of that emancipation. Western-educated Lalla Aicha not only went about unveiled, but also made speeches calling on Moroccan women "to participate usefully in the life of their country." She had shared her father's exile, the King gave Lalla Aicha the responsible job of heading the *Entraide Nationale,* the central administrative headquarters of all of Morocco's welfare agencies. The lovely Parisian-clothed Princess became a familiar sight speeding about Rabat in her white Thunderbird convertible. At Toumliline she spoke of the history of Morocco's emancipation movement and cautioned moderation in certain strongly traditional areas. For instance, she gave conditional approval to the continuation of the Moslem tradition of polygamy. Moroccan students in her audience rose to their feet sharply questioning her position. Their arguments ranged from the economic—one inheritance shared equally by several wives perpetuated inefficient small landholdings—to the romantic. The Princess retreated a little, but was in a delicate position because her father had recently taken a second wife.

In addition to attending lectures, the students spent the hot afternoons rehearsing for the many *soirées folkloriques,* studying flamenco dancing and Berber customs, or hiking down the mountain for a swim in the cold, numbing water of the spring-fed Azrou pool. There were also excursions to acquaint the visitors, and even some Moroccans, with the countryside. On the occasion of a visit to Fez most of the foreign students had an opportunity to sample Moroccan cooking and home life as guests of their newly-made Moroccan friends. The 1956 trip to the desert was repeated but this time without the political troubles, for Adi ou Bihi had been arrested and sentenced to death for leading a revolt in his province earlier in the year.

During the 200–mile bus ride to the Sahara, the students passed from the cool mountain lakes and majestic cedar trees of the Middle Atlas through the dry, flat steppes of the valley carved by the Moulouya river to the heights of the High Atlas mountain range. Here the hot travelers could feast their eyes on faraway snow–capped peaks and on the cool waters of the Ziz river as it plunged to its ultimate death in the Sahara. The road south follows the winding course of the river. The rock surfaces of the barren hills that bracket the river were wrinkled and furrowed by fierce mountain storms. By contrast the lush river banks provide irrigated life to a string of settlements, each walled and fortified against marauders. The most spectacular part of the trip was the twenty-mile descent through the winding *Foum Kheneg,* or Great Gorge of the Ziz, into the rocky edge of the desert. The walls of this canyon are variously brick-red, yellow, purple, and mauve. On the heights overlooking the gorge are a string of castles and lookout towers. For centuries their inhabitants lived by raiding the caravans forced to use this route from Tafilalet to central Morocco.

Midway on the trip, in the remote walled village of Rich, a local official to whom Father Martin had done a kindness years before, transformed the scheduled watering stop for the caravan of buses into a *diffa* complete with whole roast sheep and watermelons contributed and prepared by the tribespeople. A Moroccan Army band that had traveled 150 miles played as the Governor of Tafilalet Province greeted the surprised prior. Father Martin was moved by the peoples' hospitality for it had not been a prosperous year for them and the feast represented real sacrifices.

That night, after a swim in a desert spring, the students were guests of honor at another *diffa* in the oasis of Goulmina. The entire population of several hundred gathered around the palm grove where the guests were seated on several thicknesses of Berber rugs. They sang and danced for hours to entertain more foreigners, excepting soldiers, than had visited their oasis in its entire history. The feast lasted past midnight, when the students decided to entertain their entertainers. German *lieder,* sixteenth century Japanese love songs, Samurai laments, French peasant melodies, and a Gaelic hymn to Our Lady left their hosts a little mystified. The Americans quickly decided to give them something closer to their own music which is highly rhythmic and accompanied by intricate hand clapping. Smiling Berbers joined in the clapping to such songs as "The Battle Hymn of the Republic" and "Deep in the Heart of Texas." The Paris newspaper, *Le Monde* reported the delights of the desert people at the American professors' singing *"des melodies du Far West."*

Since there was no hotel in the tiny oasis, the guests from Toumliline slept under the stars on the thick rugs.

"The boys slept on one side of the palm grove and the girls on the other," said Father Placide, "and I slept in the middle—with a machine gun." As the rays of the morning sun stabbed into the grove they illuminated a scene which to Professor Daniel Sullivan seemed to typify the spirit of Toumliline's International *Cours*. "Without turning your head," he said, "you could see Moslems prostrating themselves in ritual prayer, a young Jewish scholar standing wrapped in his prayer shawl, and a Canadian Dominican celebrating Mass on a flat rock."

Although the lectures were an important part of the *Cours*, the most positive results were the mutual regard of Christians (Catholic and Protestant), Moslems, and Jews arising out of three weeks of close communal living. This may sound trite, especially in an age where avowals of universal brotherhood and interfaith understanding are often realized at the expense of honest and profound differences. Such sentimental feelings rarely outlast the final exotic meal or handshake. At Toumliline, however, Professor Northrop, a veteran of State Department missions to similar intercultural gatherings, was impressed by the way the differences between the groups were profoundly discussed rather than glossed over.

> By approaching the Jewish community, Islamic community, and modern French-Christian communal problems at the deepest cultural and religious level [he said] Father Martin and Father Placide have succeeded in enabling the three major Moroccan cultural groups to sit down in a common room away from the passion of politics in the quiet of a monastery to reason together. While this does not mean that all the practi-

cal, educational, and political problems were solved, it does mean, however, that each party is learning to look at the other in the light of the best traditions of each . . . *clearly the Toumliline conferences constitute one of the most constructive developments in the contemporary world.*

The Director of the Oriental Jewish Teacher's College in Paris, Emmanuel Levinas, put his finger on the reason for the climate of mutual understanding and love that existed that summer at Toumliline.

> To a Jew [he said], men alone give meaning to a place and set its tone. In the majestic Middle Atlas setting of Toumliline, it is the Benedictines who give that meaning. For several weeks, students and professors of twenty-six countries entered a society of truly free men, men who have true freedom of speech, that is, that extraordinary strength to call evil, evil, and the good, good. All dogmatics aside, here is a Jew who will say "Yes" to those Benedictine fathers.

CHAPTER 12

On THE last day of the '57 *Cours* Father Martin called together all the Moroccan participants. Meeting in one of the conference rooms off the main lecture hall, he asked them to make suggestions for next year's *Cours*. This was in keeping with the international meetings' principal aim of serving the needs of Morocco's intellectual elite. After discussion, the Moroccan delegates unanimously approved the subject of "Africa" for the summer school of 1958.

The Prior agreed in principle to their choice. He knew that the subject of a unified Africa had been one of the three most popular topics for student discussion during the two-year history of the *Cours,* the others being Moslem-Christian relations and Morocco itself. While French specialists spoke of two Africas, Black Africa, or Africa south of the Sahara, and North Africa, the African and Moroccan students at Toumliline enthusiastically discussed the unity of Africa. Living on the same colonialized and underdeveloped continent they shared the same aspirations for political and economic independence.

A graduate student in economics from the Cameroons stressed the cultural and geographical ties uniting Black and North Africa. "In coming to Toumliline for the second time," he said, "my intention was to represent to Moroccans the interest that Black Africa has in the Arab world, and also the interest that a Catholic from the Cameroons has in the Moslems of North Africa." Another student, a political exile, stressed the oneness of Africa.

> It was not without emotion [he wrote later to Father Martin] that I set foot on African soil for the first time in ten years in coming to Toumliline. While it is true that I did not travel to my own country, nonetheless I felt I had returned to my native land, Africa. For is not Africa one and indivisible? To each of her children, Africa is the very center and, to use the imagery dear to our poets, the very navel of the world.

There were more pragmatic reasons for the interest of some African students in Morocco. With their countries still under European control, they wanted to see how independent Morocco was handling its problems against the day when their own countries would face similar situations.

Father Martin knew why the Moroccans were so keenly interested in the rest of Africa. They realized that as one of the first African nations to shake off colonial control, their initial experiences at self-government were being carefully watched by the others. Further, some Moroccan politicians led by Allal el Fassi were claiming Morocco's historic rights to territory as far south as Mauritania in French West Africa. Moroccan religious leaders were actively interested in extending the Islamic penetration of

Black Africa and were inviting delegations of Nigerian and Sengalese Moslems to Morocco.

In planning the *Cours* with Father Placide, Father Martin gradually evolved the idea of an International Center of African Studies to be established at Toumliline. It would comprise a large reference and research library, several conference rooms, and living quarters for visitors. As he conceived it, it would be staffed by a permanent librarian, historian, economist and sociologist. Rather than give regular university courses, this center would serve as a meeting place for specialists, academic and governmental, to meet and discuss problems common to African nations. A minister of education from a country faced with a serious problem of national illiteracy might request a meeting with specialists from other countries who had developed effective programs against illiteracy. Economists and government officials of preindustrialized countries would attend sessions at this center to meet specialists from Europe or America.

To objections that this would simply duplicate existing facilities, Father Martin had a ready answer. Actually, there were few centers of African study. And they were either interested exclusively in a single colonial area, or were thousands of miles away in England, Canada, or the United States. And apart from geographical considerations, there were more cogent political considerations. As more and more African nations gained their independence, government leaders would be reluctant to incur the political liability of sending their men to centers of study in the former "mother country."

As Father Martin saw it, however improbable Toumliline's geographic location in the extreme north was, it appeared to be the logical place because, politically, the Center would flourish only in an independent country, as Morocco. And further, Toumliline already had the nucleus for such an institution in its own library's North African section, and in its experience running the International Summer School. Finally, Toumliline had demonstrated both its political neutrality and its ability to foster an atmosphere of good will in which genuine exchanges of opinion could take place.

Convinced of the need for this center on theoretical grounds, Father Martin saw a number of practical points that had first to be considered. What did the world's academic African specialists think of the idea? Where could the necessary funds be obtained? Finally, if there were such a center, would Africans from, say, Ghana or the Congo or Uganda make use of it? To get the answers to some of these questions, he sent his assistant, Father Placide, to the United States.

When he arrived in New York during a February snowstorm without hat or overshoes, wearing a white shirt and black tie, Father Placide looked more like a young seminarian than a veteran of seventeen years in Benedictine monasteries. In fact, he had in his pocket a letter just received from his mother in Orléans, France, admonishing him to put on his rubbers when it snowed, and to wear his scarf and button up his overcoat against the harsh climate of North America. His irrepressible sense of humor furthered the appearance of boyishness and it was a rare meeting where he did not have his interviewers laughing heartily. However, his knowledgeable discussions of North African affairs with State Department and university specialists quickly revealed another side to his character. In a letter to a friend of Father Martin, one professor at Yale wrote, "Everyone whom Father Placide met here was impressed not merely by his rare personality but also by his intelligence and wisdom."

Unlike the Prior's rambling visit of five months, Father Placide's two months stay was tightly scheduled by his American and Canadian friends. Apart from Holy Week, when he was the guest of Dom Damasus Winzen, Prior of the Benedictine monastery of Mt. Saviour at Elmira, New York, he spent four weeks lecturing in fourteen cities in nine states. He visited twelve universities and five charitable foundations to discuss Toumliline's projected International Center of African Studies. During three weeks in Canada he lectured at four universities, set up the Canadian branch of *The Friends of Toumliline* under the patronage of Cardinal Léger, and gave a series of talks on television.

African specialists in American universities were interested in Father Placide's description of the proposed Center and thought it feasible. Professor Gibb, Director of Harvard's Center for Middle Eastern Studies, and Professor Brown, Director of Boston University's African Studies Program were especially encouraging. They offered the full co-operation of their respective departments with the new Center. (The State Department sent Professor Daniel McCall of Boston University in 1958 and Professor Albert

Meyer of Harvard in 1959 to the International *Cours* at Toumliline.) One point invariably raised by the academicians was whether other African countries would profit by such a center?

This same question was raised by officials of the Ford Foundation. The only way to find out, Father Placide agreed, was to go and inquire. Accordingly an application was submitted to Ford to finance a trip through Africa to determine the feasibility of the projected center. The Rockefeller Foundation's African program was aimed more at "Black Africa," but its officials indicated the possibility of help to the center's library. Two smaller private foundations approved grants to Toumliline. One sent the Jesuit specialist on American race relations, Father John LaFarge, to the 1958 *Cours,* while the Homeland Foundation, primarily interested in the field of agricultural development, made a grant to a dairy co-operative organized by Toumliline.

One seemingly contradictory character trait of Father Placide was revealed during his American visit. This man who had developed to the highest degree the art of putting off impatient creditors and angry bankers was actually shy about asking for money. After his lectures when people came forward ready to contribute to Toumliline, he only took down their names for future membership in the American Associates of Toumliline. The money received in lecture and television appearances was consumed by transportation and living expenses. He would have ended his tour in the red had it not been for a gift from Msgr. Peter Tuohy, Director of the Catholic Near East Welfare

Association, who had helped Father Martin the previous year.

The last week of his stay was abruptly canceled when a letter from the prior ordered him back to Toumliline. The financial situation was disastrous, he wrote, and the worsening Moroccan political climate had suddenly forced radical changes in Toumliline's summer plans. As cellarer of the monastery and secretary of the *Cours,* Father Placide's services were needed immediately. His last act in New York was, rather reluctantly, to write David Rockefeller outlining the precarious financial structure of the *Cours* and asking for an emergency gift.

In London, between planes, he left information on Toumliline's plans for the Center with Darryl Forde, Director of the International African Institute. ("He wrote and approved entirely our project for a Center of African Studies," Placide said later.) In Rabat he was met by Father Martin who was on his way to Casablanca to catch a plane for Paris on a desperation fund raising mission. Driving to Casablanca the Prior got a full report from Father Placide on his American tour. In turn, Father Placide learned of the situation at Toumliline. "I discovered," he says, "that the financial situation was so bad that the Prior didn't dare write me about it. It was even *more* disastrous than when I left."

As for the political situation, Father Placide had been aware for some time of a growing crisis caused by the *Istiqlal's* drive to gain complete control of the government. In the last eighteen months the party had succeeded in gradually removing most of the non-*Istiqlal* cabinet ministers. Then, on the eve of Father Placide's return to Morocco, they brought about the fall of the government by their demand for an all-*Istiqlal* cabinet. As Father Placide discussed the situation with Father Martin on the way to the Casablanca airport, no new government had yet been chosen.

What Father Placide did not know, however, was the involvement of Toumliline in that political struggle. The Prior brought him up to date. Three Azrou students had asked to use Toumliline for *Istiqlal*-sponsored youth rallies. "I told them," Father Martin said, "that they were welcome to use our buildings but not under *Istiqlal* sponsorship, for we would not link ourselves to any party."

The Prior told Father Placide the results of a visit the very next day to Mehdi Ben Barka (a member of the Executive Committee of *Istiqlal*), to explain his refusal of the students' request. Ben Barka had accused the Prior of playing politics. Father Martin had assured him they had no political position. With his eyes flashing fire Ben Barka had looked the priest straight in the face and said, "In politics it is necessary to choose, *mon Père*."

"Ah, but we made our choice as monks long ago."

Ben Barka had then demanded that the international summer *Cours* be directed by the University of Morocco. "I told him," Father Martin said, "that I could not accept this, but I offered to let the University suggest the subjects to be treated in the summer school, beginning with this summer."

"But we have already planned this summer!"

"That is one of the reasons why I had you cut your trip short. As of now, our subject is the commune. They want us to explore the problems connected with the transition of a society based on tribal rule and custom to one based on the commune. Instead of 800 autonomous tribes, they plan to create 720 communes of from 10,000 to 15,000 inhabitants as the basic administrative and electoral unit in Morocco.

Three weeks later, King Mohammed V broadcast a royal proclamation to his people outlining the steps he would take in transforming Morocco's absolute monarchy into a constitutional monarchy. In this Royal Charter he said:

> The evolution of the country has resulted in the disintegration of the tribal structure which can no longer form the basis on which to set up representative organizations. We have therefore considered it preferable that the *commune*, which is a new social and political unit, should form the basis on which the rule of modern Morocco should be built.

The new Moroccan government of May Twelfth represented a victory for the *Istiqlal*. The only non-*Istiqlal* man in the Cabinet was the Minister of Health and he had no political ties. Two of the three Ministers who had promised funds for the 1958 *Cours* were out. Their successors added to Father Placide's financial headaches by not confirming their support until just before the sessions actually began. One bright moment in the cellarer's harassed life came when David Rockefeller sent them a gift matching his substantial grant of the previous year.

In line with Toumliline's plans for a Center of African

Studies, Father Martin reorganized the summer school. Instead of one continuous session of three weeks attended by several hundred students, he proposed four concentrated one week courses restricted to a smaller number of qualified scholars and students. But the tense international situation following the revolution in Iraq and the landing of United States troops in Lebanon almost caused Father Martin to cancel the *Cours.* Feeling was running high in Morocco and popular sentiment made it politically impossible for either the royal family or the cabinet ministers to participate actively in the sessions. The prior decided to go ahead but without publicity. There was no opening *diffa* or closing audience with the King. The press cooperated and restricted itself to a few terse announcements in place of the extensive daily coverage of the previous years. The United States was represented at these sessions by Father John La Farge, S.J. and Professors Daniel McCall of Boston University and Benjamin Rivlin of Brooklyn College.

The political and economic situation of Morocco deteriorated in the months following the *Cours.* A behind-the-scenes struggle between the right wing of the *Istiqlal* party led by Allal el Fassi and a left wing faction headed by Mehdi Ben Barka caused the new all-*Istiqlal* government to collapse in November. During the ensuing month-long crisis there were serious tribal revolts in the Rif mountains and in the hills south of Fez. It was not until late December that the King appointed a government composed largely of Ben Barka supporters, and the Royal Army quashed the revolts.

The new leftist government had been in office only one day when France informed them of the impending seventeen per cent devaluation of the French franc. Since the Moroccans had committed themselves to a program of "liberating the national economy from French economic colonialism," they refused to devalue the Moroccan currency. Overnight French capital investments in Morocco increased in French franc value by seventeen per cent. In the next few days nearly $100 million worth of desperately needed capital poured out of Morocco before effective controls were established. Half of Morocco's exports were priced out of their normal French market and the ranks of her unemployed increased alarmingly.

In conversations with the new Minister of National Economy, Abderrahim Bouabid, Father Martin decided that the 1959 *Cours* could best serve Morocco by considering the two themes "Economic Development of Pre-Industrialized Nations," and "Human Values in Economic Development." Two separate ten-day sessions in August were devoted to these subjects. Fifty-six participants from eleven countries came to the first, while sixty-eight from fifteen countries assisted at the second session.

Father Martin was pleased at the increased American institutional participation in the *Cours.* From the United States the State Department had sent Professor A. J. Meyer of Harvard. A private foundation grant administered by Fordham University sent two Jesuit specialists to Toumliline, Father Edward Duff, sociologist and editor of *Social Order,* and Father J. Franklin Ewing, anthropologist and director of Fordham's Institute of Mission Studies. A 1958

New York interview of Father Placide with the Foundation for Youth and Student Affairs bore fruit as they approved a $2,000 travel grant for students from "Black Africa." The five students, two from Dahoney, and one each from Ghana, Guinea, and the Voltaic Republic were carefully chosen by Fathers Martin and Placide. According to Prof. Meyer, they were among the most outstanding contributors to the sessions.

Three deaths in 1959, however, brought sorrow to Father Martin. On April 26, Père Albert Peyriguère died of a heart attack. This seventy-six-year-old disciple of Charles de Foucauld had welcomed the monks when they first came to Toumliline. He had shared with them his knowledge of and affection for the Middle Atlas Berbers among whom he had lived and worked for over thirty years. Father Martin had often visited the magnificently bearded priest in the tiny village of El-Kbab. He brought medicines and supplies for Father Peyriguère's dispensary because this man—perhaps the only non-Berber and certainly the only priest to become an elder of a Berber tribe—shared the poverty of his adopted people. In turn, Father Peyriguère came regularly to Toumliline for confession and to work in the monastery's library in his attempt to compile the first Berber-language dictionary.

Half of the monastic community, all that could be spared, joined the entire Moroccan population of El-Kbab in the burial procession. Archbishop Lefèvre walked just ahead of the coffin which was held aloft by ten Moslem men as they negotiated the steep alleyways of the mountain village. The plain cedar box had only two decorations:

a bouquet of flowers from the villagers and the red woolen heart and cross he had worn on his breast, the same symbol worn by Charles de Foucauld.

On Peyriguère's death, Moroccan newspapers carried the following official communique:

> His Excellency Msgr. Louis Amédée Lefèvre, Archbishop of Rabat, commends to the memory and the prayers of everyone Reverend Father Albert Peyriguère, who died in Casablanca Sunday, April 26 at the age of seventy-six.
>
> Born September Twenty-eighth in 1883, ordained a Catholic priest the eighth of December, 1906, Père Peyriguère, after teaching twenty years in the Dioceses of Bordeaux, came to Morocco in November, 1926, and from then on devoted himself with tireless energy to the sick and disinherited among the Moroccan people, above all to the Berber people among whom he lived and whose language he knew so perfectly.
>
> Tears will be shed for a long time by the tribes among whom he lived and who were profoundly attached to him. The poor above all will keep his memory, as well as those who knew the work he had done for thirty-three years to promote peace and reconciliation.

The other two deaths resulted from an accident on the second day of the *Cours*. Returning from an errand in Meknes, Madame Barbaro and Brother Jean-Michel were involved in a head-on collision with a heavy truck whose driver had fallen asleep at the wheel. Madame Barbaro, who was driving, was killed instantly. Brother Jean-Michel remained in a coma for twelve days before dying in a

Meknes hospital. Brother Gerald, the doctor, stayed and slept by his bed the entire time. Father Martin drove over twice a day to check on the condition of his monk. The loss of these two was a severe blow to the young community. Sorrowfully, Father Martin chose some land behind the monastery's kitchen garden for the cemetery and by special dispensation buried Madame Barbaro within the cloister.

Madame Edmund Barbaro, the tiny "woman in black" who had given the Abbot of En-Calcat the brown paper package of seven million francs, had a special right to that resting place within the monastery. From the moment of her founding gift till her death, she had given her life to Toumliline. During those years in Morocco she gave the monastery well over $100,000. Most of the money went for the land around Toumliline and the thirty-four acre farm of St. Benedict in the valley of Azrou. Many times she helped the monks out of embarrassing financial jams. In 1957, just before the *Cours* opened, Father Martin was in Casablanca settling a hotel bill for forty of the invited professors. He discovered he had no money. As he was making explanations to the proprietress, Madame Barbaro arrived to taxi the Prior to another appointment. Sizing up the situation immediately, she walked up to the desk, pulled out her checkbook and asked for the bill.

From the first days in Morocco, she had assumed charge of the monastery's laundry, darning the heavy woolen socks and mending the work-worn habits of the monks. They built a home for her just down the hill from the monastery, alongside the homes built for their Moroccan farmworkers.

The house was simply and functionally designed by Brother Jean-Michel in Toumliline's native field stone and cedar wood. He had also surrounded the house with banks of shrubs and flowers. Its living room was furnished from her Marseilles home and on the stone walls were hung originals of French Impressionists. From her porch, Madame Barbaro commanded a sweeping view of the hills behind and the valley below. The built-in shelves of her combination library and sewing room were lined with hundreds of books that revealed the wide sweep of her intellectual interests. Alongside the traditional French devotional writers, there were the latest works on ascetical and mystical theology. Contemporary writers and poets outnumbered the many classical authors there. One special shelf contained volumes on art and architecture which were the occasion of many discussions with that outspoken art critic, Brother Jean-Michel. These two highly individualistic persons who met death together had shared a kindred spirit. He had accompanied her to Meknes that fated day so that the seventy-year-old woman would not have to make the trip through open country alone.

The deaths of Father Peyriguère, Madame Barbaro, and Brother Jean-Michel greatly saddened the Prior. The deaths occurred just about the time that there developed a pronounced resentment against Toumliline on the part of some Moroccans. This was inevitable once the monastery became a sort of national institution, and the wonder of it is that the antagonism was not articulated sooner than it was. There was some talk that Moroccan support of the international *Cours* should be stopped. This was only talk. The resentment against the monastery can certainly be attributed in part to a Moslem disquietude at the very presence of the Church. Nothing could be more understandable, given the 1,200 years during which Christians and Moslems viewed one another with suspicion and fear. The resentment against Toumliline was especially born of the maneuverings among Moroccan politicians once their country became independent, for there were those who took an anti-French, anti-Western stance.

Perhaps the most influential of these Moroccans is the politician Allal el Fassi. Both as a theologian of Islam and as a Moslem political leader, he has preached an Islamic renaissance in the Arab world and in Morocco. In pursuit of this rebirth he has sought to discredit the impact of Toumliline on Moroccan youth. Although he was in another part of the world during Toumliline's first three years in Morocco, El Fassi discounted any assistance the monks gave the Moroccans during that troubled time. When asked if he thought Father Martin had contributed *anything* to the ultimate understanding between the French and Moroccan nationalists, he answered, "No, nothing at all." To the question did he think the monks' coming to predominantly Berber Toumliline was a French political maneuver, he replied, "Of course!" In a similar vein, he viewed the annual International *Cours* as of importance only "to certain *Roumi* (Christian) elements in Morocco." And although he cited Islam's traditional tolerance of non-Moslem religious institutions that make no attempt to proselytize Moslems, he left no doubt in the interviewers' minds that he would like to see the monks out of Morocco.

Not all Moroccans share this view. The most prominent Berber politician in Morocco, Mahjoubi, Aherdane, has been an enthusiastic supporter of the *Cours* from the beginning. "These international conferences have given us our window on the world," he said. When asked how long he had known Father Martin, he answered, "How long? I cannot tell you. When you love a man as much as I love Dom Denis, it is as if you have known him all your life."

An *Istiqlal* resistance leader in Azrou who had been in the work party outside the monastery that was given the mint tea, testified to the influence and example of Father Martin and his monks by declaring, "Toumliline helped us greatly in achieving our independence." When someone suggested this was an exaggeration, he said slowly and emphatically, "Toumliline helped us *tremendously* in achieving our independence." An Islamic theologian from the Karouine University in Fez, as rigidly orthodox as Allal el Fassi, once told Father Martin that the only thing missing at Toumliline was a mosque. "Promise me," he said with tears in his eyes, "that you will build one."

But what of the French community in Morocco? Their estimation of Toumliline is mixed. There are some whose resentment at the French loss of Morocco is transferred to the monks because they feel Toumliline identified itself from the beginning with the nationalists' cause. There are some friends of the monastery who feel that the monks have been taken in by the Moroccans. One cynical doctor, who has spent half a lifetime helping the Moslems, said, "The monks are fools. When their usefulness ends, the Moroccans will probably throw them out of the country."

Many in the dwindling French community, however, make Toumliline their spiritual headquarters. The monastery is the main retreat center for the priests of the country. Every weekend the chalets built for the *Cours* are occupied by individuals or groups of men, women, and children on retreat. On school holidays French students meet with their Moroccan counterparts at Toumliline.

Certain official attitudes were also inimical to Father Martin. There is a report in current French army files that Toumliline is actively supporting the Algerian revolution with supplies and money and is making the monastery available as a rest camp for the FLN. This of course is not true. A possible explanation for the reports may be that Toumliline has distributed food and clothing to Algerian refugees living in squalor in eastern Morocco. This work is also carried on by the United Nations, the Red Cross, and other relief agencies.

The Archbishop himself has gone on record as saying of Toumliline and Father Martin:

> I wanted Toumliline to be an example to Morocco just as the Benedictine monasteries were to medieval France. I wanted these Benedictines to be Christian witnesses of a life of prayer to an Islamic people who are a people of prayer. My expectations were great when these monks came to Morocco, and I have yet to be disappointed by them. As for Father Martin, I

> consider him an intelligent, open-minded, charitable, and totally dedicated priest and monk.

And then he gave what he considered the key to the Prior's work in Morocco:

> It is obvious that Dom Denis loves the Moroccans and is deeply concerned about their welfare. But you must realize what it is that makes him what he is: in his dealings with Moroccans, he does not pretend to be anything but *what* he is, a French Benedictine. And this is one reason he is loved and trusted by most of them.

A sharper picture of the Prior emerges when reports of criticism of Toumliline are made to him. Often he dismisses a report with a shrug and a smile. Sometimes he feigns surprise and says, "Is *that* the story he tells?" Or he asks, "Ah, but he has never been at Toumliline, so how could he really know what we are doing?" Only once did he react angrily to a canard spread by someone he had once helped. The story had to do with the political position of the monastery during The Troubles. His comment was short: "The man is a liar."

But what if the Moroccans suddenly decided that the good done by the monks was outweighed by other considerations? Dom Denis's answer to this is simple: "*Ce m'est égale.*" If the Moroccans ever decide to suppress the *Cours,* or shut down the orphanage or take away the dispensary, he says, "It's all the same to me." He regards the services of the monks as fruits of their essentially contemplative life of worship and prayer. If its interior life is in good health, he says, then all of the exterior work could be pruned away without damaging the monastery. And it was this position that prompted General Miquel to once say, "You are the only ones who will never be disappointed by what they do."

But Dom Denis explains his own case eloquently. Here is his description of their work at Toumliline:

> You would like to know what the Benedictines of Toumliline are doing? I will tell you our story. We are Christians in a land of Islam.
>
> Islam has been in Morocco for more than one thousand years. It has profoundly marked the Moroccan people. It has brought them its language, it has organized their family and civic life, it has shaped their spirits and their hearts, it has formed their religious temperament.
>
> For fifty years now men and women from France and Spain have lived among them. These people are baptized. They form a Church, the Church of Morocco.
>
> How do the two communities co-exist? How do they react to each other? Are exchanges and mutual enrichments possible? Under what conditions? To what extent?
>
> During periods of optimism the two groups would establish relations and be amazed at the facility of the contacts and at the affinities discovered in each other. Even the differences excited a sympathetic curiosity and satisfied a taste for the exotic.
>
> Sometimes periods of discouragement would follow when each group would turn in on itself; the two

spirits would be deemed irreducible. Then the thirteen-hundred-year experience (of futile contacts) in the Near East would be evoked.

A strange thing: there are self-isolated Christians living here who are ignorant of Morocco. They have lost sympathy for men. They judge they have nothing in common with Moroccans.

Is that the position of the Church in Morocco? Is it only an island cut off from its surroundings?

The answer is NO: The Church is situated on another, and more profound plane not touched by the changes of fancy. Its head, the Archbishop of Rabat, has tirelessly been teaching Christians for ten years that they have a "mission of salvation" to perform. Around him, priests and laymen are giving themselves wholeheartedly to this divine work.

This is essentially the work to which Toumliline is dedicated. I remember how, during the vespers marking our arrival, I was seized with the idea that we would offer to God the prayer of Christ in His Church for these, our as yet unknown neighbors.

These thoughts were even more intensely present during our first community Mass in the land of Islam. Moved as newly ordained priests, it seemed to us that we were exercising for the first time the baptismal power of redeeming and saving souls with our Lord. We were here primarily for that reason. Here where a people lives apparently outside of the Redemption, our task is to place them in contact with it. And even if this people, faithful to the Koran, is invincibly ignorant of this "good news," and if the pressure of their surroundings renders them effectively unconvertible, they remain capable of receiving the effects of the death and resurrection of Christ. They remain open to grace and able to lead their lives as children of God.

We understood from that moment that the principal and most efficacious means of acting in conformity with our responsibilities as Christians was the Mass. Thus, even before we had become acquainted with any of our neighbors, invisible but intimate ties bound us to them. How could we have considered them as strangers? A living mystery united us to them within a supernatural kinship.

This hidden work of redemption was completed by a more visible one. The monks lived under the eyes of the Moslem workmen with whom they worked to transform the original buildings into a monastery. We quickly realized that our actions, especially our collective actions as a Benedictine community, had value. If they recalled to Christians the sense of their life, they taught Moslems the meaning of the Church. A young man told me, "I had believed that all Christians were bad. I see now that there are some good ones." He was repeating, without realizing it, a judgment of the Prophet, who undoubtedly had been touched by a similar experience.

> "You will find that the nearest in affection
> to the true believers are men who say:
> 'We are Christians.' This is because there are
> priests and monks among them who are not
> puffed up with pride."

This verse of the Koran, cited often by our Moslem visitors, offers us a singular indication of the power of witness. If we have obtained any grace for souls, they have felt inclined to certain modes of action that example alone could reveal to them. It is necessary, however, that the witness and examples be true. The organization and the activities of a monastery manifest the Church; please God, they give an exact image, however reduced in scale. The actions of each monk shows forth Christ living in him; but it is necessary that this be Christ as He is. In order to obtain some kind of accord, to break down the "wall" separating Islam from Christianity, is it necessary to water down doctrine to form a meld pleasing everyone? Moslems would refuse it. They reject everything that is not explicitly written in the Koran. From our point of view as Christians we don't think anything worthwhile apart from the presence of Christ. His words, His grace, His salvation. "Lord, to whom would we go? You alone have the words of the everlasting." (John, 6, 69)

Shortly after our arrival, an important Moroccan invited me to lunch. After the meal he questioned me at length on our manner of living, our poverty, our celibacy, the care we were giving to the sick and to the children, our prayer. Then he asked me, "Why do you do all these things?" I answered him simply: "We are trying to continue on earth the life of Sidna Aissa, Our Lord Jesus." He did not pose any more questions. He had understood.

Are the Moslems a little anxious about our presence? From the first days of our foundation, important people of the countryside came to Toumliline to meet us and to ask what we were doing. I must say that these anxieties and suspicions are not yet completely dispelled. When one speaks of the children we are bringing up, of the co-operatives we are trying to organize, or even of the International Summer School, they ask what we hope to accomplish ultimately. That is why frankness seems to me preferable to silence, which would leave the field wide open to doubt and misunderstanding. Let them be reassured. We respect absolutely the liberty of souls, freedom of conscience. But we would not be servants of God if we remained indifferent to their salvation. Whether they be Moslems or Jews, understand that we envisage the problem solely within the perspective of our Christian faith, in the manner I have just briefly sketched. Are our Moslem friends astonished at this point of view? Not at all. They do the same thing themselves when, in order to signify that we are truly religious, they tell us, "You are true Moslems."

As for the Christians, I wish they understood me completely. I recently had the opportunity to present these ideas to a group of French Christians of a nearby town. Their reactions surprised me. They concluded, not without a certain peevishness, "You have come, therefore, to Morocco for the Moslems and not for the Christians." I asked them in turn, "In what I have just related to you, show me what separates us from the Christians?"

The monastic life? The monk is only a Christian who takes the steps to be more perfectly faithful to the obligations of his baptism. The aspiration to perfection ought not in itself to distinguish him from other Christians. It ought to be common to them all. But he has chosen certain means put at his disposal by the Church in order to accomplish this more quickly and more surely.

You object, what about the cloister! The cloister has as its only aim to shelter the monastic community from the contaminations of "the world." It does so in order to constitute an entirely Christian city, whose goals, spirit, organization, and activities are governed exclusively by evangelical principles. You find that this city is opposed to the one in which you live, which you are tempted to call the true city? Yes, without a doubt, to the extent that the latter is not inspired by Christ. For the Christian, the monastery ought to be a kind of pilot city. It stands there apart, to recall to him what ought to be the essential orientation of his milieu.

Thus our open contacts with Moslems, far from opposing us to the Christian community in Morocco, unites us profoundly to it. The problems posed by our situation as Christians in a land of Islam are common to all of us. Equally members of Christ, we have in Him the same vocation, the same responsibilities, the same work of salvation to accomplish, the same glory to procure for God.

On November Twenty-third, 1959, Father Denis Martin, Father Edouard Le Bel, and Father Jacques de Charry drove to Casablanca and boarded the ship *Jean-Mermoz.* Eight days later they reached Abidjan, the major port of the Ivory Coast Republic on the West coast of Africa.

The monks drove north through a tropical jungle. A hundred miles beyond Abidjan the jungle ended and a vast savanna stretched before them. Stunted trees and yellow grass and dead blue volcanos rose up against the silver sky.

After another eighty miles the Benedictines entered the city of Bouaké. Here they were welcomed by a representative of the local bishop. Five miles beyond the city the monks came to a small, abandoned stone building located on a rise of land dominating the savanna.

Father Martin and Father Le Bel said good-by to Father Jacques de Charry. The Prior promised he would send two other monks as soon as he reached Morocco.

Toumliline had created its first African foundation.

> We come to Bouaké [Father Martin said] in the same spirit in which seven years earlier we came to Toumliline. With no preconceived ideas or definite plans, we come simply to lead our monastic life, to draw down from heaven God's blessings on this country.
>
> We do not come in great numbers. Our wish is African vocations to our Benedictine life so that soon this Ivory Coast monastery will find its proper African personality. Then, faithful to the desires of St. Benedict, the monastery will be a house of hospitality, offering to all who come peace and refreshment. Above all, it will become a house of prayer.

INDEX

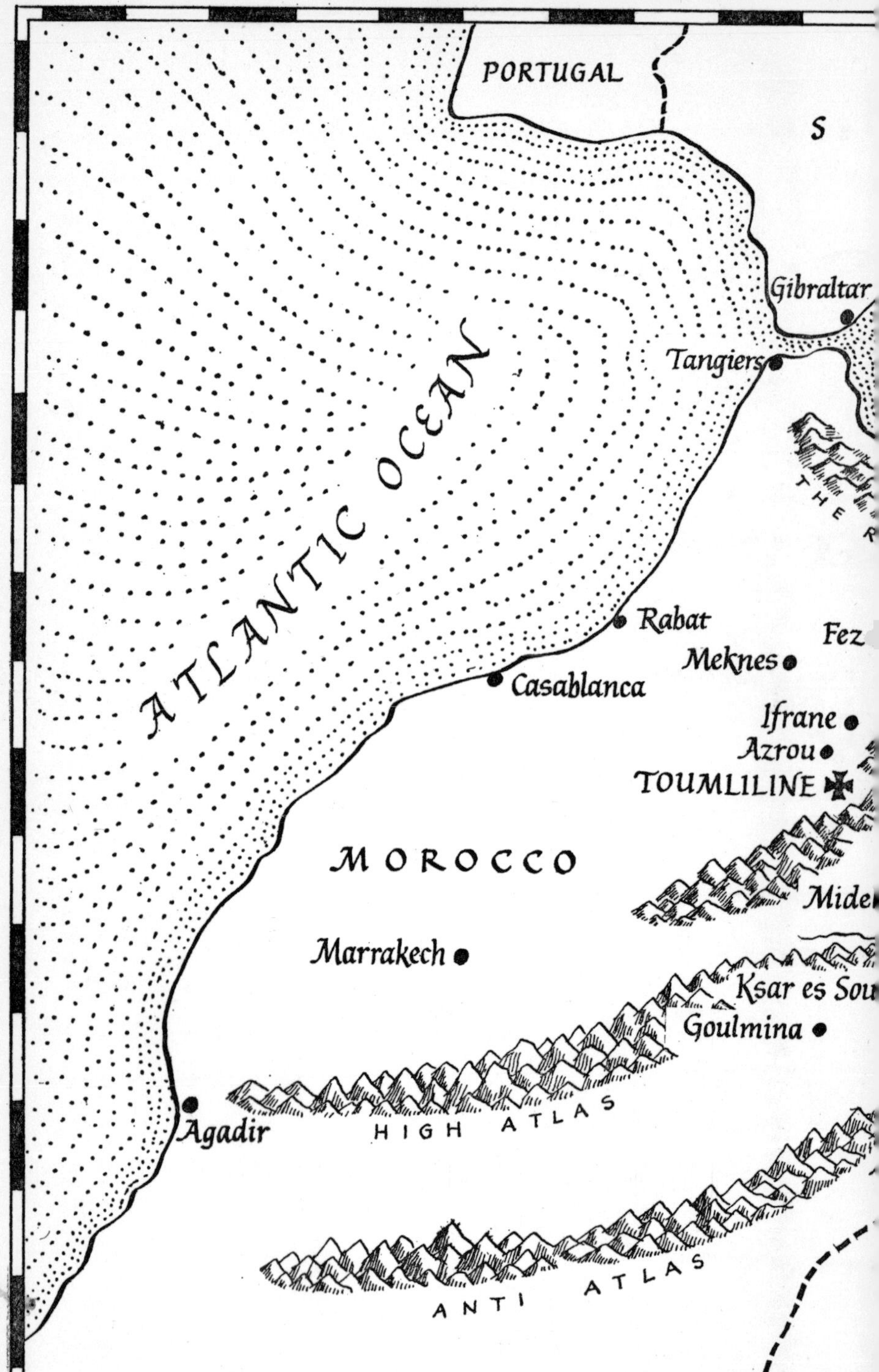

PORTUGAL

S

Gibraltar

Tangiers

ATLANTIC OCEAN

THE R

Rabat

Fez

Meknes

Casablanca

Ifrane

Azrou

TOUMLILINE

MOROCCO

Mide

Marrakech

Ksar es Sou

Goulmina

Agadir

HIGH ATLAS

ANTI ATLAS